THIRD EDITION

THE RESEARCH TOOLKIT: PROBLEM-SOLVING PROCESSES FOR THE SOCIAL SCIENCES

By Bruce D. Friedman

Bassim Hamadeh, CEO and Publisher
Kassie Graves, Direcotr of Acquisitions
Jamie Giganti, Senior Managing Editor
Jess Estrella, Senior Graphic Designer
Amy Stone, Field Acquisitions Editor
Claire Benson and Rachel Singer, Associate Editors
Elizabeth Rowe, Licensing Coordinator
Joye Lue, Interior Designers

Cover image copyright © Depositphotos/r.Hilch.
          copyright © Depositphotos/bluehand.

Printed in the United States of America

ISBN: 978-1-5165-0862-4 (pbk)/ 978-1-5165-0863-1 (br)

CONTENTS

Preface ix

1 | **What Is Research?** 1

Understanding Science
Types of Research
Cognitive Research Map
The Research Process
Evidence-Based Practice

2 | **The Question** 15

Types of Questions
Descriptive
Relational
Causality
Interaction

Evaluating a Research Question
Research Question Worksheet: Select a Researchable Question

3 | **Literature Reviews** 23

Defining Literature Reviews
How to Search
How to Do a Literature Review

Where to Search—Demystifying the Databases

Boolean Logic

Reading a Research Article

    Abstract Construction

Writing a Literature Review

Literature Review Worksheet: Literature Search

Hypotheses

4 | Justification of the Study   37

Who Cares?

Relevance to Who Cares?

Do I Need the Right Answer?

Alternative Answers and Their Implications

Justification Worksheet: Justifying the Study

5 | Variables   41

Types

Operationalizing

Variable Worksheets

6 | Research by Numbers—Descriptive Statistics   45

Levels of Measurement

Graphs

    Figure Bar

    Figure Histograms

    Figure Frequency Polygon

Ages of Respondents

Characteristics of Distribution

    Standard Deviation

    Negative Skew

    Positive Skew

Measures of Central Tendency

    Mean

Estimating Mean

    Median

    Mode

Identifying the Mode

Central Tendencies in Distributions

Measures of Variability

Tabled Data

Variability

Standard Deviation

Properties of Standard Deviation

Range

Descriptive Statistics–Applied Example

7 | Hypotheses   65

Types of Hypotheses

Directional

Non-Directional

Hypothesis worksheet: Hypothesis or Purpose for the Research

8 | Research Design   73

Experimental, Qualitative, Mixed Method Research
Experimental Research Designs

Random Assignment

Pre-Test/Post-Test

Randomized Subject, Pretest Post-Test Group Design

Solomon Three-Group Designs

Solomon Four-Group Designs

Reliability and Validity

Threats to Internal Validity

Overcoming Threats to Internal Validity

Threats to External Validity

Overcoming Threats to External Validity

Eliminating Procedural Bias Worksheet
Reliability
Factors Affecting Reliability
Standard Error of Measurement
Confidence Intervals Using SEMs
Improving Reliability

Survey Research

    Steps to Survey Development

    Designing Questions

    Evaluating Questions

Action Research
Research Design Worksheet

9 | Sampling   103

Quantitative Sampling Techniques

    Random Sampling

    Stratified Random Sampling

    Cluster Random Sampling

    Systemic Random Sampling

    Non-Probability [Non-Random] Sampling

    Convenient Sampling

    Purposive Sampling

    Quota Sampling

Qualitative Sampling
Sampling Worksheet

10| Protection of Human Subjects   119

Belmont Report
Protection of Human Subjects Worksheet

11| It's All about Relationships—Inferential Statistics   125

Correlations
Chi Square and T-Tests
Instruments and Data Collection Worksheet
Code Books
Data Collection Form Worksheet: Instruments and Data Sources

12| Qualitative Data   139

Patterns of Discovery
Looking for Patterns
Sources of Data
Collecting Interview/Focus Group Data

Analysis
Mapping

13 | Reporting Results   147

Journal Article Outline
Force Field Analysis
Logic Model
Reporting Results Worksheet

Conclusion   153

References   154

Preface

Aburning question has always been the relevance of academic material to real-life situations. This became more evident when I began to think about why many social science students seem to have an aversion to research. Having worked for a number of years before returning to earn my PhD, I saw how funding agencies, particularly United Way but others as well, were interested in the evidence for the effectiveness of the services that were provided. Thus, it was incumbent on me to identify ways to measure the outputs of the services that were provided to see if they aligned with the outcomes or the goals that were anticipated.

However, given the practicality of being able to assess my own practice or the practice of the agency as a director, it did not change the nature of the perception of coming into a profession where the goal is to help others. Did the required research courses relate to the ability to assess the effectiveness of the services that we provided? Upon entering my doctoral program, I looked at the textbooks that were being used to teach research. They had a lot of conceptual information about the research process and statistics, but how could I translate that to practical aspects of my professional life, especially in understanding how to evaluate the effectiveness of my practice interventions?

This became more complicated when I arrived at the dissertation phase of my doctoral studies. I was working with the homeless collaborative in Fairfield County, Connecticut, in the 1980s, when society was experiencing a growth in the number of people who were homeless. The collaborative wanted to build more homeless shelters, but I asked a question: what happens in the homeless shelter to address the problems of people who were homeless? This led to the development of what I classified at the time as a qualitative study but would now be identified as an explanatory sequential design mixed methods study (Creswell, 2015) within a community-based participatory research (Hacker, 2013) framework. What I realized at that time was that there were not many funding agencies that were willing to fund qualitative studies. This meant that the system was driving large sample studies to do hypothesis testing, but not really studies that could be used for decision-making. This became somewhat frustrating because the nature of the science and information in the 1980s around homelessness and homeless services was not as sophisticated as it has become over the past thirty years, and there needed to be room for identifying answers that would contribute to being able to make decisions on how to specifically address the problem.

Thus emerged the development of The Research Tool Kit: Putting It All Together as my effort to integrate research methods into practical applications that can be used in the social sciences to try to bridge the gap between hypothesis testing and research for decision-making. Whereas most research courses were conceptual on research methods, The Tool Kit was designed to provide a practical tool that partialized the research process into a step-by-step approach that could be used in designing a method for all research, from evaluating one's own practice to understanding population trends and their implications.

The Tool Kit has evolved over the years from being a simple workbook to providing more techniques for developing decision-making research projects. This became most helpful as I began teaching a research methods course within an Educational Doctorate program for Educational Leadership. Thus, my experience was not just from a social work practice perspective, but now also understanding educational research. I also had a stint working with practicing physicians on the medical school faculty and began to apply these same concepts with them. The practicing physicians began to see how the research tools were helpful for them in varying aspects of their practice, including how to search the literature in a timely and effective way to help them understand evidence-based practice. Thus, the tools provided in this third edition have been tested not only in my host profession of social work, but also in education and medicine, and found to be useful for them in developing more practice-based research.

This also relates to the comment above as to how research methods have changed since the first edition was published in 1997. Originally, research was classified as either quantitative or qualitative, and now we are looking at a variety of research that includes both quantitative, qualitative, and mixed methods. Prior, most research was done to test hypotheses. Now research has developed into hypothesis testing, various action research methods, and program evaluation. Thus, the field of research has become more sophisticated as our practice has developed. In addition, there are greater accountability demands on the nature of our practice. Some of this is a result of economic factors, but more importantly, there has been a growing demand to understand how and why things work the way they do. In addition, there is a growing demand to answer the "what can we do?" question to arrive at solutions. Thus, this *Tool Kit* is more important than ever. It does not provide all the nuances and details of the concepts about research and statistics; one will still need to reference more comprehensive sources for that. However, what this Tool Kit does provide is a structure for developing and applying the research process to practice.

I realize that research may sound like a scary part of a curriculum, but by breaking it down into manageable steps that can be applied to your own practice, to understanding population trends, or whatever your research needs might be, research becomes a tool for practice and is not scary at all. This *Tool Kit* can be used when you are working with a single subject, with a group of people, or trying to understand systems change. Thus, this is a very practical tool in helping to conceptualize and develop a research protocol, including how to present information to the Institutional Review Board for acceptance.

There are a number of people that I want to acknowledge who have both been helpful in the development of this product as well as my understanding of the research process. I need to thank my research faculty, who helped me understand methodology and conceptual development of research to practice. Thank you Claudia Coulton, Thomas Holland, Howard Goldstein (z"l), and Art Naperstek (z"l) for providing the foundation that I needed to make this project a reality. I would like to thank Karen Allen for her use of these pages in completing her own dissertation. I also want to thank my doctoral students who have also used these pages in the designs of their own dissertations. Most importantly, I want to thank my children, Jaron and Bryan, and my grandchildren, Ben, Sam, and Madison, who have taught me the importance of keeping it simple. It is easy to get caught up in the jargon of the profession or research, but it is a lot harder to keep things simple.

I would also like to thank Lisa Gebo (z"l), who believed in me enough to sign the first two editions of the *Tool Kit*. And most importantly, a thank you to Kassie Graves, who saw the value of the *Tool Kit* for it to be published by Cognella.

What is Research?

The term research is sometimes scary for students, and it is something that they try to avoid. When one hears the term, there is the association with numbers and tables, scary things for someone who just wants to help people. The term is honestly associated with a form of scientific inquiry that relates to everything we do. Research is a thought process that one uses to problem-solve. Research is a method of inquiry used to build knowledge. In essence, research is a scientific process used in every aspect of our lives. The scariness comes from the association that has evolved around the term research. The physical sciences have used the term research to relate to large number sets with large statistical probabilities. Many students shared the reason for going into the human service field was to avoid the math associated with the large statistical sets. Some of your experiences in science or mathematics may have been unpleasant, therefore leading you to pursue an educational path in social sciences. The reality is that research is a logical thinking process that builds knowledge. We all do research every time we solve a problem. The large number sets that one associates with the mathematics of research is really arithmetic or solving equations. Mathematics, on the other hand, is truly a logical thinking process or the theory behind the numbers. Research should be associated with the mathematics, or logical part of our everyday life, and not with arithmetic. This book provides a practical, step-by-step approach to the logic of research. It is through the logic that one is able to develop a practical application to a problem-solving process that helps integrate practical, life experiences into a scientific method of inquiry.

Understanding Science

Science is built on two different realities: what is observed and what is agreed upon. What we observe is not always what is agreed upon. The difference between the two creates a sense of two different types of reality in the world.

These two types of reality lead to two different views of the world. There is the static view, or what is built upon facts and knowledge. These facts and knowledge are based upon an interrelated set of propositions about particular observations or a particular set of empirical phenomena. Empirical phenomena are observations that have been tested again and again. For example, when we let an object fall from our hands, we are aware that it will fall to the floor. We call this principle gravity and understand how it works after repeated observations of letting things drop from our hands and seeing them fall.

Since there is agreement about these observations, acceptance that is based upon both logical and empirical support, then these observations lead to propositions. Propositions are used to help explain events in nature. When these propositions are recurrent, we can use them to predict what we should be observing. We call these **theories**. If these theories predict things almost all the time, then we would call them **grand theories**. The reality is that there are few things like gravity that explain things most of the time. As a result, we have a number of **mid-range theories** that predict things some of the time. In the social sciences, we are happy if these explanations occur around 20 percent of the time. Thus, that provides a lot of space between what we observe and whether that observation is supported by what we see.

As a result, what we observe does not always match the anticipated observations. We begin to see a discrepancy between what is observed and what the set of propositions tells us should be observed. This leads to a dynamic view of science based on process or activity. This process or activity then leads to a need for further observations. These additional observations are analyzed to see if there are logical explanations for them. If we can identify logical explanations for the observations, then we look to see if the theory is faulty or whether we have a new theory or explanation for the observations. The inconsistencies in these observations lead to **empirical generalizations**. For example, the 1980s saw an increase in the number of homeless people. The early literature placed the problem on a lack of affordable housing and the gentrification of America's cities (Reamer, 1989). The solution was to build more affordable housing. However, the problem of homelessness persists and has even expanded. There was a need for additional observations to understand what other factors were contributing to the rise of the homeless problem (Friedman, 1994). These additional observations led to a number of factors contributing to the exacerbation of the homeless problem. Such factors as access barriers to the support systems that were developed to prevent homelessness or the closing of the mental institutions without adequate community support have contributed to the growing homeless problem in addition to the lack of affordable housing. These additional observations led to **empirical generalizations** about the reasons for increases in the number of homeless persons. As these empirical observations become more prevalent, then we can build theory.

In addition, these empirical generalizations led to the development of policy factors. Thus, President George W. Bush felt that homelessness could be eradicated in ten years and encouraged communities to create plans for eradicating homelessness in order to receive funding. One of the problems was that the definition used to define who was homeless was not consistent with the evidence of who was actually homeless. Thus, the ten-year plans were initially identified as successful since those individuals who were the most chronically homeless were the ones targeted rather than the situational or the episodic homeless. As the economy continued to get worse and the inequity between rich and poor increased, more families and individuals were becoming homeless. Thus, the empirical generalizations were not keeping up with the realities of society.

The relationship between theories, hypotheses, observations, and empirical generalizations is depicted in figure 1.1. This cycle demonstrates a scientific process that is interactive with one building on the other. This development of science, especially in the social sciences, is a constant ebb and flow where repeated observations are used to build empirical generalizations that lead to theories that predict hypotheses that are tested by observations. The process of using the theories to create a probability statement that explains the relationship between certain phenomena is called developing a **hypothesis**. This cycle is called the **inductive/deductive** cycle of theory construction and relates to the struggle between knowing and building knowledge. The inductive side uses observations to build theories that explain events in society. The deductive side uses the theories to draw conclusions that explain how things should work.

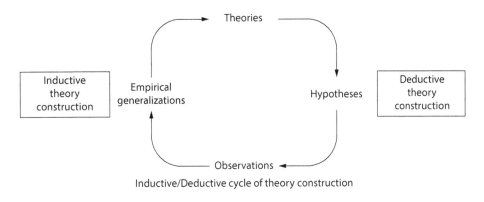

Inductive/Deductive cycle of theory construction

FIGURE 1.1 INDUCTIVE/DEDUCTIVE CYCLE OF THEORY CONSTRUCTION

For a variety of reasons, the state of social sciences is not at a point where the theories can explain what happens in society. Because our theories do not consistently explain events, we need to adapt the theories based upon our current observations to try to get a better understanding and explanation of events in the world. Thus, social sciences are considered a young science with very few theories that explain phenomena. Instead, the social sciences consist of a number of small or mid-range theories that explain parts of phenomena. This leads to a struggle between forms of scientific inquiry and is called the quantitative/qualitative research debate. It also relates to the social sciences taking parts of different theories to explain certain aspects of a phenomenon and parts of other theories to build on other parts of the same phenomenon. Thus, within the social sciences, it is easy to see how multiple small or mid-range theories are used to understand and test a particular phenomenon.

Types of Research

The quantitative research method emphasizes the production of precise and generalizable statistical findings (Rubin and Babbie, 2014, pg. 79). This method is used when the theories dictate the nature of the observation to be observed. The theories create hypotheses that are then tested.

Qualitative research methods emphasize understanding. To return to the homeless discussion above, there was the question of trying to understand why there was an increase in the number of people who were homeless. One could not ascertain why, so one had to ask probing questions to find out why. This method involves a less precise exploration of finding and a more global process of inquiry to formulate understanding of problems. These formulated assumptions are then tested in a more rigorous manner. The goal is to understand the observed phenomenon in order to lead to theory development.

A **theory**, then, is a set of concepts that describe the interrelationship between these concepts. It is the interrelationship between the concepts that leads to the ability to predict events. Theories then provide clues or suggestions for interventions. We use theories to help explain things that we do not understand. Theories are used to help us organize agreed-upon observations or facts about some particular phenomenon. A theory has three main functions: to organize, to explain, and to predict. The three functions of theories lead to the development of hypotheses. Going back to the gravity analogy, then, we know that if we are holding something and then let it go, it will fall and hit the floor. Gravity provides an understanding of the concept that a smaller object will be attracted to a larger object; in this case, the item being held will fall toward the earth.

Thus, theories help organize the information about a particular event. Once the facts of the event are in an organized pattern, then theories help to explain the event. This knowledge is used to then predict future occurrences of similar events. Therefore, when a baby begins dropping things from his/her high chair, they fall to the floor. The baby quickly learns that dropping or pushing something off the tray will cause it to fall. Now if the parent quickly retrieves that item, the baby learns that if something drops while mom or dad is there, then they will have a reaction of them picking it up. Thus, gravity is explaining what happens to the item dropped from the high chair tray, and there is another observation that the baby has about mom or dad's behavior toward dropping the item. This demonstrates that there are times when more than one theory is used to explain a particular event. This is especially true when the event is a new experience or phenomenon, like when babies begin learning how to get what they want. When theories are used to predict the relationship between two or more concepts, it is called **hypothesis building.**

A **hypothesis** is a statement describing the relationship between two other concepts. The relationship is logically derived from existing theories. The hypothesis then predicts the observations from the interactions between these two concepts. Hypotheses are expectations about the way things should be in the world if the theoretical expectations are correct. Thus, our baby has learned that when they drop something from the high chair tray, mom or dad will pick it up. However, if mom or dad does not act the way the baby expects, then the baby has learned another behavior to attract attention to him or her to get what he or she want—crying. Thus, babies are hypothesis building and testing from the moment they are born, and that is part of the learning process.

Just as babies test hypotheses, as scientists, we also test hypotheses, albeit a little more sophisticated than when we were babies, as part of the research process. The scientific process is an ingrained process to our learning. We quickly learn that the hypothesis predicts a direction or expresses an assumed relationship between variables. It is the observation of the relationship between these variables that is used to determine whether the hypothesis is correct or incorrect, and if incorrect, then we make an adjustment to our hypothesis to try to get it to work.

The reality is that nothing, not even gravity, is accurate 100 percent of the time. Therefore, a hypothesis itself is not tested. As scientists, we test the inverse of the hypothesis, which is called the **null hypothesis**. This may be an irrational thought process of not wanting to discredit what we already have observed, so we test the opposite, and by discounting the opposite, we can then infer or suggest that our observation is correct. Thus, the scientist hopes to find sufficient evidence to allow for rejection of the null hypothesis. The disproving of the null hypothesis then suggests the opposite to be true. In addition, it also means that we are not proving something since there are very few absolutes; rather, we suggest that there may be some truth to the presumption suggested by the hypothesis. This way, we keep the scientific aspect fluid by suggesting implications and not proving by fact. Just a word of caution: hypothesis testing is more about testing relationships between variables as suggested by theories and not about decision-making. There is a significant difference in the type of research one does when focusing on decision-making rather than hypothesis testing. This will be discussed in chapter 8 when action research components (Participatory Action Research and Community-Based Participatory Research) are introduced.

The process just described is another way of expressing the deductive approach to theory construction. As stated earlier, not all relationships between concepts have been explained by a theory. Since the social sciences are still young, there continues to be many relationships that are not explained with theories. In addition, many of the theories that currently do exist are not strong predictors of the relationships. Therefore, the nature of the world in the social sciences is to build theories. Glaser and Strauss (1967) call this the discovery of theory from data—which they call grounded theory (pg. 1). In other words, *grounded theory* is an inductive approach to theory construction.

By inductive approach to theory construction, the researcher analyzes observations that lead to empirical generalizations. There are no theories that predict relationships, so the researcher observes the interactions between concepts in order to see if there are any repeated events. The repetition of these observations then suggests some generalizable relationship. From this process, the researcher then develops a theory. However, since there are no existing theories that predict relationships, this form of research is called **exploratory research**.

Besides exploratory, there are two other types of research that the researcher needs to think about. They are **descriptive** and **explanatory**. Briefly, descriptive research records and reports the interaction between factors, regardless of the causal relationship. Thus, descriptive research describes what is being observed. Explanatory research confirms or explains the relationship that previous research has described. The explanation of observations is done through statistical measures and thus is quantitative in its approach. Since qualitative research is more open and relies more on observation than precise and generalizable statistical findings, then qualitative research will primarily be exploratory with the possibility of some descriptive research methodologies.

There will be more about these types of research later in this chapter. Before moving to the discussion on these types of research, it is important to understand the cognitive development of research and then describe the process that an individual follows in performing a research project.

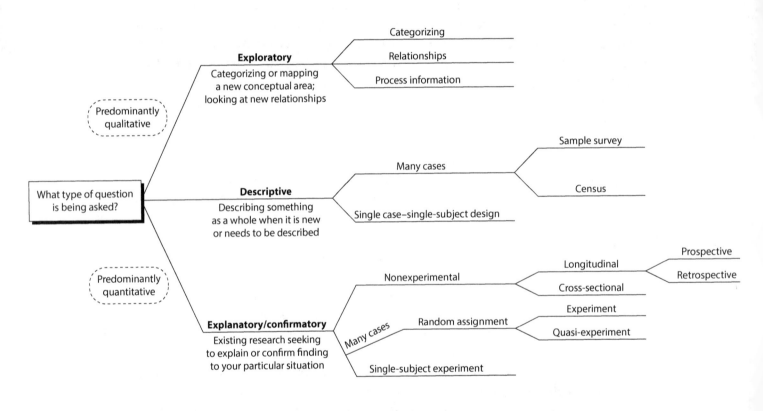

FIGURE 1.2 RESEARCH DESIGN DECISION TREE

Cognitive Research Map

Research begins by trying to answer, define, or explain a problem, interest, or an idea of the researcher. The researcher then looks at the theoretical concepts that relate to the problem. A **concept** is a mental idea or representation of a class of events or group of objects. Concepts are words that symbolize ideas that have been created by the researcher. For example, if I tell you to close your eyes and visualize a car, each of you will visualize some type of car. However, if I then asked you to describe the car, the answers that I would get would be very different depending upon who was responding. Some of you may say '57 Chevy, while others may say a red Corvette, and others may say black BMW. What this points out is that if the concept of "car" is mentioned, everyone seems to have a sense of what the concept means; however, when it comes time to actually describe that concept, there is a lot of variance. Thus, concepts are invented by the researcher. It is then important for the researcher to **operationalize** the concept by developing a precise definition.

In thinking about the problem, the researcher identifies a couple of theoretical concepts. What the researcher then begins to do is to look at the relationship that exists between these concepts. At this point in time, these concepts are very abstract; it is hard to observe the concept because the definition of what is being observed is not precise. Just like the car, the researcher has not defined what is being observed, so the observation is obscure.

Returning to the homeless question mentioned above, the basic definition of a homeless person is someone without a home. However, there is a tremendous variance as to what that means. Is a battered woman who leaves her home to escape the abuse homeless? Is a minor who runs away from home homeless? The person who was burned out of their home is obviously homeless, but what about the person who was evicted because of insufficient money? And what about the person who is doubled up because he or she cannot afford a place of his or her own—is that homeless? This identifies differences in individuals, but there are also differences between individuals who are homeless and homeless families. Before beginning any homeless research project, it is important to clearly define what is meant by homelessness and who is homeless. Thus, it is important to clearly define the terms that are being used. This is true for every research project.

To **operationalize**, the researcher clearly defines the concepts and the relationship between the concepts. This is accomplished by assigning measurable terms to the concept. For example, a black 528i BMW or an individual who has not lived at any particular address for thirty or more days are ways of beginning to operationalize car and homeless person, respectively. When the researcher has been able to clearly define the concepts, the researcher has created a **variable**. A variable is just a concept that can be measured.

Since problems are really questions about the relationship between concepts, the researcher needs to understand the nature of the relationship in question. The researcher is faced with looking at two or more different variables that have a relationship with each other. The researcher is left to describe the nature of the relationship.

For example, in thinking about services that address the homeless problem, the homeless shelter comes to mind. But what is the homeless shelter? To operationalize it, a homeless shelter is an emergency, temporary residence that provides room and board for an individual for no more than ninety days. This clearly differentiates individual shelters from family shelters. It also clearly defines the transitional nature of the shelter rather than that of a residence. To study the relationship between homeless people and an agency that serves them, the two operational definitions of homeless people and shelters would be used to begin to explore relationships between the two.

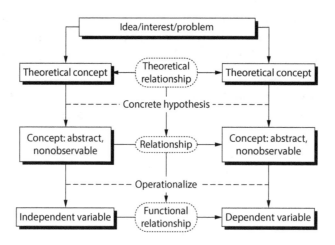

FIGURE 1.3 COGNITIVE RESEARCH MAP

A way of understanding the relationship between variables is like baking a cake. One needs the raw ingredients like eggs, flour, sugar, and water before starting to bake a cake. These raw ingredients are mixed in a bowl, put into a pan, and baked. The result is a cake. The cake analogy describes a relationship between variables. The eggs, flour, sugar, and water are all the **independent variables**. By themselves, they stand alone. When mixed together, there is an interaction effect that creates a cake. The cake, then, is dependent, or the **dependent variable** in the study. There are also some control variables. These controls are the size of the pan, the length of time the batter is mixed, the baking temperature, and the length of time in the oven. In addition, there may be environmental factors that could confound the outcome of the cake. For example, most recipes are written to be made at sea level. However, if one lives a mile above sea level, then adjustments to the recipe need to be made in order to obtain the desired outcome. All these become factors that relate to the quality of the cake. As you see from this example, there can be a variety of extraneous factors that may be at work in achieving the desired results.

A research question is just like baking a cake. A relationship exists between variables. It is up to the researcher to determine which are the independent variables and which are the dependent variables. Unlike a cake, however, sometimes the relationship is not as clear. This is where the conceptualizing takes place and the need to sit back and reflect on the meaning of the question. The cognitive process of developing a research problem is represented by figure 1.3.

Returning to the homeless example described above, the two concepts are homeless people and homeless shelters. If the outcome is that people become housed, then the independent variables become the homeless people and the homeless shelter. However, "becoming housed" needs to be clearly defined. In the case of an emergency shelter, "becoming housed" could mean just getting the person off the streets and providing them with basic shelter and food. On the other hand, if one is defining "becoming housed" as a permanent transformation of an individual's housing situation, then one needs to understand all the steps that are involved in permanent housing. The transformation of the homeless person to one of "being housed" then becomes the dependent variable. The vehicle to achieve housing is through the supportive services that are offered by homeless shelters. However, these services may not be identified, and the needs of some groups of homeless individuals may be different than the needs of others. Thus, the identification of services to achieve housing would be a question that this study may want to explore. In essence, the services would be independent variables, but since they are not identified, then it is important to do exploratory research to identify what those variables are.

From this brief example, it is possible to see that independent and dependent variables are not clear in some social science questions. In addition, the type of research (exploratory, descriptive, or explanatory) will determine how you look at the relationship between independent and dependent variables. That is why it is important to understand the cognitive nature of research within the context of the research process.

At this point in time, it might be important to discuss the relationship between variables and how one defines those variables can influence the nature of the research process. What comes to mind is the relationship between substance abuse and mental health. The question is whether substance abuse causes depression, or is the person using substances because it is a way of self-medicating oneself from the issues associated with having a mental illness?

The Research Process

To this point, there has been a discussion about research as a form of scientific inquiry that provides a methodology for answering questions. However, there has been no discussion about the research process. Figure 1.4 depicts the research process. From the figure, we see that there are two processes that coexist. One is the logical and cognitive process, and the second is the technical process of doing research. The logical and cognitive process involves the first two steps of choosing a problem, defining the question to be answered, identifying the variables that relate to the question, and forming a hypothesis, if possible, to look at relationships between variables. If variables are missing, then one needs to do an exploratory study to identify what those variables are. The rest of the research cycle is technical. This cycle is applicable for both inductive and deductive approaches to research.

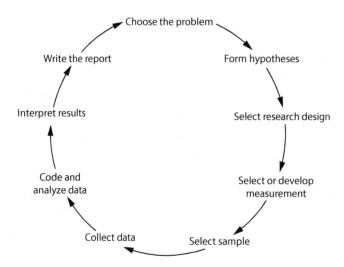

FIGURE 1.4 THE RESEARCH CYCLE

As previously stated, research is conducted to answer a question. Therefore, to begin any research process, one is faced with a question or a problem that the researcher wants answered. The problem may only be relevant to the researcher, but that is all right since it is the researcher who wants to find the answer. The researcher is left with determining how to find an answer. As stated earlier, there are two different realities in life: that which is observed and that which is agreed upon. The researcher looks at the question/problem that s/he wants answered and begins a search of existing literature to determine whether the state of knowledge appropriately or adequately answers the question or problem at hand. If the researcher feels that the existing literature is sufficient to answer the question, then the researcher chooses the deductive approach to testing the question. However, if the researcher determines that the level of knowledge does not adequately answer the question/ problem, then the inductive approach is followed. It is important to understand that most research questions are not a simple one or the other, but usually a combination of the two. Where the qualitative/quantitative debate arises is more in design methodology, which will be discussed below.

The next step is to identify the causal relationship between the variables, or which ones are the independent and which are the dependent variables. If the causal relationship is clear, then you have formed a hypothesis. Regardless, it is still important to go through the process of operationalizing the concepts that relate to the problem in question. Once the concepts have been operationalized and turned into variables, it is then important to identify the relationships that exist between the variables. Since a hypothesis is a statement that defines the relationship between variables that can be tested empirically, it is important to describe the nature of the relationship. However, there are times when you are not sure about the nature of the relationship. Then you have a study without a hypothesis to test. This is an exploratory study. Figure 1.2 is a quick look at the nature of the question and how it would translate into a specific type of research study.

Referring back to figure 1.2, it is important to first understand the nature of the question being asked. To understand the question, the researcher goes through the logical and creative process of the research cycle to fine-tune the question and the formulation of a hypothesis. In the likelihood that the question represents a new conceptual area, then the formulation of a hypothesis is not possible, and the researcher chooses an exploratory research design. Exploratory research involves a systematic process of observations and then analyzing the observations to see if there are generalized categories that describe the relationship between variables.

In the likelihood that the researcher is able to describe a relationship between variables, then the researcher chooses a descriptive type of research design. Descriptive research is used when the researcher can identify relationships between variables, but the relationship is still new. Therefore, the state of the art is to describe the relationship. The researcher can do this in several ways, but usually through some type of survey or census of many cases or by conducting single subject design. Single subject design is a case study method that is clinically based for the experimental study of single cases (Barlow and Hersen, 2009). The experimental nature tests relationships that are suggested through the hypothesis. In either survey research or single subject design, the focus is to describe the nature of the relationship that exists between variables as described in a hypothesis.

The third type of research question is explanatory or confirmatory. This is where the researcher has determined that there has been sufficient research to explain the problem, but the researcher wants to confirm how generalizable the existing research is to her/his specific question. Therefore, the research confirms the results of existing research in relationship to the specific question that is being addressed.

As you can see, the logical process is necessary to determine the nature of the technical process of research that will follow. That is why literature review is placed very early in the process since it helps the researcher determine whether there is sufficient information to develop a hypothesis or there is inadequate existing research and the need for conducting an exploratory study. In addition, the literature review is an integral part of the logic to research and should be started early in the process. However, the literature review is a continuous process that should be checked throughout the entire research process. A warning, though: there needs to be a balance between literature review and actually carrying out the study. Researchers can sometimes become complacent waiting for someone else to answer their question and never fully have their question answered. That is why I call research a passion, for the researcher is truly following her/his own passion for obtaining an answer to her/his question. The conceptualizing is difficult, but once that is decided, then the rest of the research process is purely technical. There is some art to the technique, especially in a qualitative study where the interpretation of the data or data analysis is very much dependent upon the researcher, but that will be described in Chapter 8.

Now that the researcher has gone through the mental gymnastics of identifying the existence of causal relationships and formulation of a hypothesis or identifies that there is insufficient research to support hypothesis testing, then one can confidently determine a research design. A research design is simply the development of a procedure for collecting and measuring the data. Again, these next steps are techniques that will vary depending upon the type of research design selected. Later in this text, I will go through the specific techniques as they relate to your research. There are numerous other texts that describe other research techniques as they relate to research studies. The methodology for collecting/measuring the data is subject to the rigors of validity and reliability testing that will be discussed in chapter 8.

Once the criterion for collecting/measuring the data has been determined, then the researcher decides on the sample frame. This is the selection of the subjects from the population who will help to answer the question being asked. Again, there are a variety of factors that relate to sampling. Many of these will be dictated by the nature of the question and the type of design that the researcher chooses.

Now that all the headwork has been completed, it is time to collect the data. This is simply the operationalizing of the study. Again, this is very much dictated by the nature of the research question and has been outlined throughout by the researcher in the development of the study. More detail will be provided in chapter 7.

The next two steps will vary dramatically depending upon whether the study is exploratory, descriptive, or explanatory. Remember, descriptive and explanatory studies have a hypothesis that is being tested. Therefore, the data that is collected can be coded and analyzed in a way that proves or disproves the hypothesis. Exploratory research does not have a hypothesis that shows relationships between variables. Therefore, the coding and analyzing of the data are very different. It is from the analysis of exploratory data that relationships between variables emerge.

This leads to the interpretation of the data. Again, the nature of interpretation will differ on the type of research. Descriptive and explanatory research will interpret why or why not the relationship happened the way it was hypothesized. Exploratory research will use the interpretation to suggest relationships that will lead to hypotheses that can be tested by descriptive research.

Finally, it is important to write a report. For what good is the acquisition of new information if you are only going to keep it to yourself? The purpose for doing research is to acquire new information or to solve a problem. Since you were solving a problem that concerned you, then you could assume that someone else was probably also concerned about the problem. Therefore, it is important to share your discovery with the world. As stated earlier, the nature of knowledge in the social sciences is not complete. There are still many unanswered or incomplete questions. Therefore, it is important that we share our knowledge to be able to build knowledge within the social sciences.

There is an additional school of thought that research needs to have an action step to it, for what good is gaining the knowledge if it is just going to sit on a shelf somewhere without any action being taken to change the situation that led you to perform the research in the first place (Sagor, 1992)? Research should be done to improve a condition that exists; thus, it is important to include action steps that will be taken once the information is obtained. More information about action research, participatory action research, and community-based participatory research will be discussed in chapter 8.

The research cycle is just that: a cycle. The nature of research is to answer questions and to share our knowledge with others. One type of research builds on another. Exploratory research is used to identify the relationships between variables. Descriptive research describes the nature of the relationship more fully. And explanatory research confirms the generalizability of the relationship to the larger population. Therefore, it is a continuous cycle where new knowledge leads to new questions that someone wants to answer. That is why I do not like the terminology of qualitative/quantitative research debate. Research methodology is not a debate but different ways of gaining knowledge. One method is needed to build on the others. There is an ebb and flow between the two methodologies that needs to be understood.

Evidence-Based Practice

There is another component that one needs to consider in conducting a research project. That is the evidence that the information will make a difference. Within the human services, there has been a lot of discussion about evidence-based practice or best practices. The thing that becomes important in understanding is whether the information gathered will make a difference in improving the lives of the client systems that we serve. Figure 1.5 below shows the nature of evidence-based practice. There is the current state of literature or knowledge about a problem, there is the current state of the client circumstance, and then the client system's values and expectations. These three domains are intersected by the values and expertise of the service provider (worker). Thus, the worker's intersection of these three domains becomes a best practice model about how one defines evidence-based practice. Granted that there continues to be opportunity for the worker to gain additional growth and knowledge to be able to expand the best practices available, hence the need for continuous learning experiences.

The balance of this text provides you with a step-by-step approach to complete a research project. Not that it is the correct way, but research is a logical process. As in any logical process, if the task can be partialized into manageable steps, then there is a greater likelihood that the goal will be achieved. Therefore, this text is a way to make the task of doing research manageable.

One last thought before getting started. Research is not a separate, isolated discipline but one that is integrated throughout social work practice. The steps presented here are very similar to the steps followed in working with client systems in identifying solutions to problems. The steps may not be so specifically spelled out; however, the process is the same as that of working with client systems. For example, when you are doing an intake, you are actually gathering data. An assessment involves defining concepts and operationalizing them. A literature review is done by looking

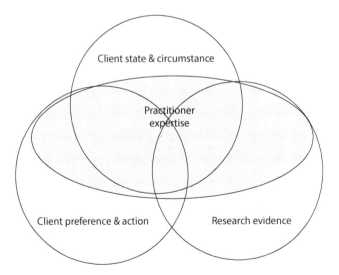

FIGURE 1.5 EVIDENCE-BASED PRACTICE

at other cases that may be similar to the one being presented. Contracting and performing an intervention is the same as conducting a research project with the ability of measuring the results to determine whether the intervention was successful. Therefore, research is just a technical term for our interactions with client systems. We may have different definitions for client systems, albeit micro, mezzo, or macro forms of practice, but research is a systematic approach to the work we do with them.

The Question

The most important and yet the most difficult part of any research study is developing a researchable question. One does not begin a research project by stating the type of research that s/he plans to conduct; rather, the type of research is dictated by the nature of the problem that is being addressed along with the nature of the existing knowledge to address that problem. It is through the development of the question or problem that leads the researcher to making the decision about the nature of the research design.

A research question can derive from any problem that seems to exist that the researcher wants answered. One begins by stating the problem in the form of a question; however, unlike the television show *Jeopardy*, stating a question is a thoughtful process that encompasses many nuances and will most likely evolve as more information is learned about the topic. Thus, stating a question involves refining and developing the question further. The development of the question is a process in itself and should not be perceived as something that is complete the first time it is asked. It is all right to change and refocus the question as more information is uncovered about the subject.

Broadly stated, a research question is a general statement that indicates the purpose of the study or the issue that will be addressed. The research question includes parts that inform readers of the:

- study focus or purpose
- key variables or outcomes
- target population
- study methodology

Another way of thinking about it is that a good research question includes information about the five core "W" questions:

- What is the problem, and how often is it happening?
- Where is it happening?
- Who is engaged in the behavior?
- When is the problem most likely to occur?
- Why is the problem sustaining?

Some examples include:

1. What conflict resolution strategies are most effective for reducing marital conflict?
2. Does one-on-one therapy promote the adult social learning skills within a domestic violence perpetrator more than participation in a batterers intervention group?
3. Does job training promote the occupational skills of individuals with disabilities?
4. What factors contribute to teachers' sense of collective self-efficacy related to improving student learning outcomes?

As shown, the research question identifies the problem/issue at hand and identifies key variables and in some instances the target population. Although research questions should include the main variables of interest, it is commonly up to the individual(s) conducting the research to specify the target population in the actual question. As you will see in published research in your respective field, there are many types of research questions and many styles in which they are written.

Nonetheless, a research question should be a clear and concise statement with no unnecessary wording. Therefore, the aim of consumers of research is to understand the types and components of research questions.

Types of Questions

The main characteristic of the research question is to frame the purpose of the study at hand. To ensure the relevance and substance of a question, it should be considered in light of existing literature/information to see if it has been answered or not. There is no reason to address a question that has already been answered. Instead, it is more desirable to build on the information on a given topic, such as the effect of parental beliefs on students' academic achievement, to develop a new, untested question. Information gathered on addressing the new question will then help fill in the gaps about what is not known about the problem/issue at hand.

Meltzoff (1998) identified four types of research questions:

1) Questions of description

Questions of description deal with learning about the characteristics of individuals in which data was collected or exists for one or more population subgroups. Some examples include: the average math performance of sixth-grade students at a particular school; incarceration rates of men and boys of color; quality of life of patients who experienced different types of organ transplants; level of reading motivation among third-grade English Language Learners. In each of these cases, the aim of the question is learning something about one or more groups in which data was obtained.

2) Relationship questions

Relationship questions seek to examine the extent to which certain variables vary with one another. For example, the question "Does reading motivation predict English Language Arts (ELA) performance among third-grade students?" or "Is substance abuse a predictor of chronic homelessness?" are examples of relationship questions. In these instances, the researcher seeks to gather evidence on the relationship between higher levels of reading motivation as it relates to increased ELA performance or the relationship between substance abuse and incidence of chronic homelessness.

3) Causality questions

Causality questions seek to address the effect of one variable on another. They are similar to relationship questions except there is a specific direction in asking how one variable influences the other. For example: "Between Cognitive Behavior Therapy (CBT) and Solution Focused, which therapeutic intervention is more effective in decreasing conflicts among married couples?" In causality questions, the way in which one variable (therapeutic intervention) directly leads to changes in another variable (marital conflict) is of primary interest.

4) Interaction questions

Interaction questions are similar to causality questions but focus on the degree to which the impact of one variable on another differs across population subgroups. For example, the question "Does PBIS (Positive Behavior Interventions and Supports) improve school culture adequately to improve academic outcomes for all students, including those who would be classified as at-risk?" is a causality question that focuses on the degree to which PBIS may function differently across student groups (all students versus those identified as at-risk). However, it differs in that the question seeks to determine whether the effectiveness of PBIS may differ across learner types. A finding that PBIS may benefit normal students more than at-risk ones may provide the basis for modifying the existing program to incorporate other behavior management tools such as restorative justice or peer mediation or even a combination of all three to better serve a broader range of students.

As shown, there are many types of research questions to begin the process of scientific inquiry. The ways in which these questions guide research will be discussed throughout. The aim here, though, is to illustrate the different types of questions that can be posed. Each type of question is unique, and the sort of question(s) to ask depends on the interests of the individual asking the question. Therefore, no question type is "more correct than the other"; instead, the type of question to ask just depends on one's interests and the information that exists on the topic in the existing literature base.

Evaluating a research question

Selecting a research question relevant to one's discipline is challenging. It requires the use of (a) one's prior knowledge/experience with the question, (b) existing literature/information, and (c) information to justify the most appropriate approach to addressing the question. Factors to consider when developing and evaluating a research question are:

1) Relevant and substantive.

This means that the question is directly related to the current state of research/practice and is meaningful. It would not serve you or the field much use to answer a question that is out of date, as there would be little interest. This is one of the main reasons to consider professional wisdom and review published research related to one's research question(s).

2) Not answered.

This factor relates to ensuring that the research question is relevant and substantive. In this case, a research question that you want to investigate should not have already been answered. If considerable evidence has been accumulated that seems to answer one's research question, then it is important to ask what other dimensions of the question have not yet been answered. The aim here is to shed new light on a different aspect of a problem. There is no reason to reinvent the wheel. Thus, there may be factors that could be addressed relating to specific population groupings, geographic differences, or urban, rural differences between what has already been answered and whether those findings relate specifically to what you want to know.

3) Contributes to existing knowledge.

Indeed, if someone is going to dedicate countless hours to gathering evidence to answer a given question, it would be hoped that the answer would contribute to the knowledge base. This factor relates to the importance of thoroughly evaluating the information that exists on one's topic to see where the existing gaps are, or those areas in which more information is needed. As such, the evidence gained to understand an issue should promote the theoretical knowledge on a topic and promote practice. It is also important that once you find an answer, you are willing to publish it. For if you answer a question but then do nothing with it, then how is it contributing to the existing knowledge?

4) Personal interest.

Probably one of the most important factors to consider when coming up with a research question is one's personal interest toward the topic. Given that research is a self-motivating endeavor that requires the dedication of countless hours, it is imperative that one is interested in the topic. Why spend time investigating a question if you are not interested? In this case, then, the research question should relate to one's "burning interests"—what is it that you really want to know more about? This also indicates that the research question be based on one's passion. Have you ever wondered why there are so many people who begin doctoral programs but fail to complete them? Could it be that there was not the passion in the research question to motivate the individual to finish?

Although many factors contribute to a research question, there are many things to consider when developing and evaluating a research question. What is your "burning question"? Let me demonstrate by using a practical example from the qualitative research about homeless shelters that I performed. While in the Bridgeport area, the community began experiencing an increase in the number of homeless people. The initial reaction was to build more homeless shelters to house all the homeless people on the streets.

However, a range of questions arose in trying to address this social problem. These included: "Who were the homeless people?" "What is the nature of the system that should be developed to address the homelessness problem?" and "What happens in a homeless shelter to address the problems that led to the person being homeless?" The problem related to a causality between a service delivery system, homeless shelter, and a particular population group, people who were homeless. However, within each of these concepts, homeless shelter and people who are homeless, there needed to be a refining of the terms to make them operational. More on operationalizing variables will be discussed below. However, from a theoretical basis, it was presumed that the service delivery system, homeless shelter, would address the needs of people who were homeless, thus looking at more than a generalized relationship but more on the causality of one variable on the other, thus driving the research process to explore some possible answers to the causal nature on the relationship between these two variables. Therefore, the questions or problems that one wants to obtain direct the research.

In the study mentioned, the initial interest was to build homeless shelters to warehouse people. Once people looked beyond the actual bricks and mortar of the facility and began to understand true service delivery, then there was the development of an exploratory question that showed causality between the variables: **"What happens in a homeless shelter to address the problems that led to the person being homeless?"**

Let us further dissect the question to see how it relates to a research project. First, look at the question. It is clearly stated in the form of a question. Therefore, there is a problem that we are trying to gain information about. Second, look at the terms in the question. There is the term homeless shelter, people who are homeless, and problems relating to the condition of being homeless. Before beginning any type of research, these three terms have to be defined to gain an understanding of the current state of knowledge in this area. For the sake of this research, I defined the terms as follows: Homeless shelter was part of the social system that provided food and shelter for people who did not have a home or a place to reside. People who are homeless were defined as single adults who did not have a permanent or temporary residence in a given twenty-four-hour period. Problems relating to the conditions or situations that led to why the person did not have a residence included a variety of things, such as lack of employment, substance abuse, mental illness, or a combination of factors of substance abuse and mental illness, and many more. Since this was exploratory, many of the issues were not really known, and part of the process was also to try to identify what some of those factors may have been. As it turned out, there were a number of adverse childhood experiences that occurred in the person's life that could have been contributing factors to being homeless as an adult.

By beginning with these general definitions of the terms, I was able to begin the next phase of the research: to conduct a literature review to see the state of information relating to the question. Let me point out that these definitions and the question were just preliminary steps. Through the process that I will describe, these points will be refined into an operational approach to conducting a research study. The following page provides an outline for you to develop your own research question. Remember, state the question/problem that you want answered in the form of a question. Look at the question and identify the themes to the question and then define those themes. Below is a form that you can use to begin thinking through your questions in order to help with moving forward to developing a research project.

SELECT A RESEARCHABLE QUESTION

Begin by stating a question of great interest to you in a simple, non-technical interrogative sentence.

_____
_____
_____
_____

Does the question address the five W's of: "What is the problem, and how often is it happening? Where is it happening? Who is engaged in the behavior? When is the problem most likely to occur? and Why the problem is sustaining?"

Identify the important terms in your question and define them using as concise language as possible.

Terms	Definition
1. _____	1. _____
2. _____	2. _____
3. _____	3. _____
4. _____	4. _____
5. _____	5. _____

Literature Review

Now that you have stated a research question that possesses several desirable properties of who, what, where, when, and how and determined whether the question is descriptive, relational, causal, or interactional, it is important to understand the existing knowledge that relates to our question. First, we seek to identify the terms that we are using; hence the reason for identifying and defining terms. Then we need to see if there is a relationship between two or more of the terms to determine relationship, causality, or interaction. Since that process was begun in the previous chapter, it is possible to see what previous theory and research provide to determine the merit of the study and what variables to focus on, among other things (e.g., methodology).

This process leads us to consider the existing body of knowledge as it relates to our particular problem/question and how our research question fits within the context of the existing knowledge on the topic. In particular, if a research question has already been addressed, one's research question should build on this acquired information. Thus, a research question should be original and one that will lead to future research while being of interest to you as the researcher. Also, because we typically do not have unlimited resources at our disposal to study a problem of interest, addressing the issue should be within the abilities of the researcher. These include factors associated with time, money, and any other resources. Remember the KIS (keep it simple) principle. The more complex the question, the longer it is going to take for you to arrive at an answer and the longer it will take for you to complete, so **Keep It Simple**.

Last, one must consider the ethical factors associated with addressing a particular question. Associated with this consideration is ensuring for the confidentiality and well-being of those who participate in a study.

Defining literature reviews

With all of this in mind, it is possible to begin the next step in the research process, the literature review. Different people may suggest doing the literature review at different points in the research process; however, I believe that literature review is an ongoing process that should be included throughout your research. Therefore, I begin the literature review very early and will periodically expand the literature as new information raises new questions.

In order for a research question to develop from a broad statement to one that is researchable, a careful, thoughtful review of the existing body of literature needs to be completed. The literature review is the process associated with searching, identifying, evaluating, synthesizing, and tying together the body of research on a given topic. The aim of searching and gathering relevant research is to enable you to gain an understanding of the current level of knowledge about the problem. The review of the literature will enable you to gain an appreciation of the variables involved with the problem (or how other researchers have defined those variables) and identify the ways they have addressed them in order to guide future research around similar issues. Other factors associated with conducting a literature review include:

- Allows you, the researcher, to identify boundaries of what previous research has done and found related to your research question.
- Enables you to review theories and research related to your specific research question or puts the research within a current context.
- Allows you to further define and refine the concepts addressed in a study.
- Shows what others have found to help you with expected results for your study.
- Identifies which methodologies have been shown effective and which seem less promising.
- Avoids the problem of unnecessarily duplicating a previous study.
- Provides the basis for interpreting your results; that is, what are the implications of your findings in relation to previous research findings?

How to search

The downside is that there has been an explosion of accessible information. With this explosion of information, it is easy to become deluged by the literature. Therefore, the literature review works hand-in-hand with your research question as the question helps to focus on what it is that you want to find. There may be times when the literature will sidetrack you onto other topics. Then it is important to ask yourself whether this new question is more interesting than the one you began with or whether you want to remain with the original question. That is why it is necessary to continually refer back to your research question when conducting your literature review. A strategy that I use is to write my question on an index card and tape it to my computer as I search. As I read the abstract, I continually refer back to my question to see whether the study is addressing my question or not. If so, then I continue reviewing the article. If not, then there are two things that I may do: either save it for future reference or discard it as it is not relevant to my interests.

How to do a literature review

There are a number of issues related to your question that you hope the literature will answer for you. First, you want to know whether someone else has already answered your question. If your question has been answered and you are satisfied with the way that the research was conducted, then there may not be any reason for you to continue with this particular question. In most cases, there may be similarities to existing research but your specific question was not answered. In the case of the homeless shelter question, there was research on defining characteristics of homeless people, but there was no research that specifically looked at the homeless shelter.

Second, once you find some research that is similar to your question, then you want to identify the theories or models that were used by the other researchers to answer their questions. Recall from the first chapter that theories provide a framework for predicting observations. Therefore, it is important to identify the theories that other researchers used to explain their observations to see if these same theories are applicable to your question. Again, in the homeless shelter study, two competing theories emerged. One was social systems theory, which looked at the shelter as part of a larger social system to address the needs of homeless people. The other theory was social support theory, or the negation of social supports that may be contributing factors to why people become homeless. This then led to a theoretical framework that explored the issue of if a homeless shelter, as part of the service delivery system, was able to build social supports, then one could presume that the long-term factors associated with chronic homelessness would be addressed. However, there was no information about applying the combination of these theories to homelessness at that time. This then led to looking at other populations where the interaction of these two theories had an effect on changing the outcomes of the population. What came to the forefront was the system of aging services in order to assist the elderly population to continue to age in place, or the ability to continue to live independently in the community, and what services needed to be provided to assist in that process. Thus, for this study, there was no specific theoretical framework that had been used, but by looking at ancillary populations and applying those theories, it was possible to create a theoretical framework that could be tested with a new population group.

Third, you look at other research to see what other questions may have emerged from their research. The issues of poverty and joblessness continued to emerge as contributing factors to people being homeless. This became an important element to consider when looking at the role of the shelter. These other factors helped to differentiate between types of shelters that serve different populations; for example, there are different services needed for single adults (both men and women) compared to family-oriented shelters compared to domestic violence shelters or even youth emergency shelters. All of these are emergency shelters, but because of the differences in population needs, it was important to redefine the service system being studied. Remember the KIS principle; it is important to understand your resources and limitations, so make things easy, and the literature review can help identify that potential. For ease and simplicity, then, the literature helped to redefine my population to study only shelters providing services to single adults. A number of other factors also emerged as factors to consider from the literature. For example, the issue of racism as a factor of homelessness continued to be suggested by the literature. This was identified by questions that identified more people of color as being homeless. Thus, other factors relating to your question may be identified through the literature review, and in my study, they included issues of race, gender, class, and identity.

Where to search—demystifying the databases

This is all well and good, but how do you begin to do a literature review. As children, we are taught to think what I call "horizontally." By that, I mean that we are taught to address questions very broadly. Our first piece of elementary school research was to look up a word in a dictionary. Then we graduate to using an encyclopedia as a reference tool. By definition, both dictionaries and encyclopedias provide an overview of many different topics. They do not go into depth. That is sufficient for early research projects, but we are in a professional program trying to dig more deeply to be able to arrive at solutions to problems. To do that, it is important to dig deeply and not broadly, or to think vertically rather than horizontally. Well, before we can think vertically, it is important to understand the horizontal surface. By that, I mean we have to understand the concepts that we want to research. We started that process by defining our terms in the research question. But what do those terms really mean? Most professions have published dictionaries that are specific for the profession. Thus, looking at the respective professional dictionary is a good place to begin to see how the profession is defining the terms of your study. For social work, there is *The Social Work Dictionary* and the *Encyclopedia of Social Work* as good places to begin to get a general understanding of your research question. For education, there are the *Encyclopedia of Educational Research, International Encyclopedia of Educational Evaluation, American Educators' Encyclopedia, International Encyclopedia of Education: Research & Studies, International Higher Education: An Encyclopedia, and Review of Educational Research* (AERA), to name a few. Psychology also has *Annual Review of Psychology and the Encyclopedia of Psychology*. These are just a few examples of some of the general professional resources that you might use to help with defining your terms within the professional milieu of the context of your study. There are others, and many times it is important to look at multiple professional sources since each problem cuts across professions, so professions may define things differently depending upon the context.

As just mentioned, the research process within professional programs expects us to be able to think vertically. By that, I mean a process that involves narrowing and focusing on the question until we find the answer that satisfies our level of inquiry. The deeper we dig, the more information we find out about the problem. There will be points along the research process that will answer parts of the question; that is fine, for it may satisfy you. However, to continue the quest, there needs to be a passion or desire to find the answer that will satisfy your particular question. There is no one dictating when to stop; only you know when you have identified a satisfactory answer. There may also be side questions that emerge, as previously mentioned. That is why it is important to keep your question in focus. You may find that one of the side questions is more interesting to pursue than your original question. That is fine as well because it is your question.

The literature review in the homeless shelter research was very helpful for me. It helped me narrow my understanding of the search by narrowing my population (single homeless individuals) and to narrow my definition of the service delivery system (shelters serving single adults). That is why I said in the earlier section that the question is not complete but is something that you will develop as you gain more knowledge and information about the subject.

To begin the narrowing process, use the dictionary, encyclopedia, and thesaurus to obtain basic definitions and identify key words that relate to your question. This will not answer the specifics associated to your question but only provides a foundation on how to begin. That is why the literature review is begun early: to help with the narrowing and focusing of your research.

Once you have used dictionaries, encyclopedias, and thesauri to identify key words, then you move to an intermediate step of looking at other background sources of information. This may include looking at your textbooks or other general books on the topic. You may also look at some annual reviews or other general information such as newspapers or popular magazines. All this will help you gain a clearer understanding of how to address your question.

Once you feel that you have a good understanding of your question, it is possible to move to other sources of information retrieval. There are many types, including bound copies of abstracts and bibliographies on the subject that you are researching. However, technology has also affected the way we can find information. There are now easily accessible electronic databases that will help you search many volumes of information in shorter periods of time. Online, electronic databases, typically available on your home computer through a library or free access source, provide perhaps one of the most useful places to gather published research (e.g., articles, books) on a particular topic. Such databases provide the opportunity to search for articles and other published information (e.g., conference paper) based on key words and other filters (e.g., specific years and intended audience). A perusal of your library's electronic database demonstrates the various disciplines in which electronic databases filled with articles exist. A few of the electronic databases here exemplify databases that contain articles related to some social science research, including: Educational Resources Information Center (ERIC), Psychology (PsycINFO), Medicine (PubMed), Nursing (CINHAL), InfoTrac, ProQuest, and Ebsco Host (general library databases). As previously mentioned, the first four are discipline-specific, and as such, the thesaurus for each database will help with the appropriate terminology and definitions for the terms. There are many other databases to explore. In addition, there may be a variety of databases that have information about the subject that you want to research. However, be careful that the terms mean the same for each database. For example, in searching homeless in PsychInfo, the citations identified causative factors to people being homeless. Sociology abstracts identified social forces leading to homelessness. ERIC identified children coming from homeless families. And MedLine identified citations on medical issues relating to homeless people. Therefore, some thought needs to go into the search before you begin. That is why it is important to keep your question visible and start with the question. The important thing is that since you are doing scientific research, it is important to identify a database that abstracts peer-reviewed articles and not general information.

A peer-reviewed article is one that has been submitted to a journal and has been reviewed by other scholars for accuracy prior to it being published. This is where the other scholars would review for accuracy to determine whether the content is evidence-based. Different journals subscribe to different abstracting services (sometimes multiple abstracting services) that publish the abstract and sometimes full text copies of the articles that have been published in the peer-reviewed journals that contract with each service. Thus, when citing a piece of someone else's work, it is important that the research has gone through a peer-review vetting process to ascertain the research accuracy of the article's content.

Some web searches are done through various web browsers. A word of caution here, though. Most of the material that one finds on the web is not peer-reviewed and thus not evidence-based.

Thus, a general web search for your question may identify a number of items, but those items are not peer-reviewed and may not be useful to help you with your research. There is, on the other hand, a generalized search tool that does review peer-reviewed materials. Google Scholar (is it important to include the scholar) does provide a generalized search of peer-reviewed manuscripts and may be a place to gain an understanding of the quantity and quality of the literature that already exists on a particular topic.

These can be very helpful, but a word of caution. One should not just sit down at a computer terminal and punch in key words without first having looked at the specific thesaurus for that abstracting service. An example is the term "social work." Most electronic abstracts would see that as two words, social and work. As such, the database would find all citations that included both words, though not necessarily the phrase "social work." The search would then follow that pattern of citations with both social and work. What you identify would probably be off the mark of what you want to find. Therefore, it is important to include the appropriate identifiers for that abstract that would search for "social work."

Boolean Logic

As previously mentioned, the amount of information available on any particular topic may be overwhelming. Therefore, it is important to develop a good search strategy and an even more important way to store the articles that you do choose to reference when developing your own study. First, let me talk about developing a good search strategy. Your research question identified a few key words. The key words are a good place to begin. If there is a causal relationship between the key words, the order that the key words are entered is also important as well as how you use your Boolean logic. I will cover Boolean logic in a minute, but first I will address the order of the words.

The way a computer search works is that on the first pass through, the database uses the first word in the search protocol, eliminating everything that does not include that word. Then the computer searches the remaining database for the subsequent words. Hence, order is very important.

When you apply Boolean logic to the search process, the second and subsequent passes through the database do one of three things. Boolean logic uses one of three operators to link key words. The operators are AND, OR, or NOT. Thus, during the first pass through the database, the computer identifies everything in the database that contains that word. Depending on the operator that is used, AND will narrow the database by identifying the use of both terms together. OR will increase the database because it will identify the other word as a synonym to the first. NOT will limit the database because it identifies the first but not the second. Thus, Boolean logic is an important way to identify the literature that specifically relates to the information you are seeking.

Another limiting factor to the search process is to limit the search period. Unless specified, a search will involve everything that has been written on a particular subject. However, you might only be interested in looking at information from a particular date. For example, when thinking about understanding the issues of homeless shelters, the homeless issue was not identified as a problem until the late 1980s. Prior to that, the literature describes homelessness in relationship to migrant farm workers with a lot of information coming from Cornell University School of Agriculture. Thus, if you are not interested in some of the historical aspects of the problem, then you can limit your search to the 1990s to current. And if you want to look at the homeless issue since the development of President George W. Bush's implementation of the Ten-Year Plans for communities, then you can restrict your search from 2005 to the present. This process of knowing the dates that relate to your specific problem will help reduce the number of articles that will be identified by the various databases. Another approach if you are not sure about the specific time-line relating to your problem is to begin gathering the most recent articles and work backward, such as locating articles published within the last five years and moving to earlier years. Beginning with the latest published research will provide a basis to determine the current state of research in a field—that is, what research problems are researchers and theorists now addressing?

This does not mean that earlier content is of no value. As stated above, there are theories that relate to how a problem is being addressed. Therefore, it might be important to search those theories separately to see how they are used and can be integrated into the literature that you will use for your study.

Reading a research article

Now that you have conducted your search and you have identified hundreds of potential articles that relate to your question, it is important to develop a strategy on how to determine which of those articles are keepers, which need further investigation, and which to eliminate. Follow this process to determine whether an article may serve useful. First, consider the title of the article. Does the title include the key words that you were searching? Does the title describe the relationship of those key words, and how does that relate to your research question? If there is no relationship to your question, do not spend time on the article, eliminate it. Second, peruse the article's abstract.

Abstract construction

The abstract is a brief (about 150–200 word) description of the study, its findings, and implications. Factors in the abstract may include: research question(s), description of study participants, experimental design, general findings, and implications of results. If the abstract indicates that the study is directly related to your interests, a brief skimming of the article will allow you to judge whether it is worth saving and using in the literature review. Factors to consider include, among others: clarity of literature review for justifying the need for the study, representativeness of the sample to the target population, methods of data collection and analysis, and lastly, implications of study. Consideration of these factors will enable you to see how they are addressed across diverse studies related to the research question. If the article does not address your needs, eliminate it. Thus, you have employed a process of how to review literature in a timely way to determine what is relevant to your study.

Here is an example illustrating the process of using a research question to search for published studies using the ERIC electronic database. The guiding research question is: "How do student athletes adjust to a university setting?" Potential key words to use in one of the electronic databases to gather relevant articles include, among many: student athlete, college adjustment, transition, anxiety, time management, and satisfaction with university.

Obviously, the goal of the literature search is to gain an understanding of how this question fits into the existing literature. It also provides a basis to learn about: (a) what previous research has been conducted on a topic of interest, (b) how variables are defined and measured, (c) methods to investigate the question, and (d) areas in which more information is still needed. Some things to gain out of a literature search include, for example:

— what research has been done on the topic
— what has been the target population(s) of published studies
— what methods have been used in the research on a topic
— what are the main variables and how have they been defined and measured
— practical implications of study findings, among others.

Results of the ERIC literature search yielded thousands of relevant articles, books, papers, etc. As shown here, this search included journal articles, conference papers, and bibliographic information. This search also provided a conference paper by Hurtado on Latino Student Transition to College: Assessing Difficulties and Factors in Successful College Adjustment from 1994. The study was published in the peer-reviewed journal *Research in Higher Education* in 1996. If one was to decide which Hurtado resource to obtain for one's references, it would be recommended to select the peer-reviewed journal article over the conference paper. This is because the published study in the journal will report the complete study, which was reviewed by two or more experts in the field. While informative, studies reported in a conference paper do not typically undergo the thorough review conducted by peer-reviewed journals.

Another strategy to limit the amount of information provided by a search is to just focus on locating peer-reviewed journal articles and exclude books and conference papers, among other sources. Articles from peer-reviewed journals are strongly recommended to guide one's literature search, as they contain studies based on a blind review by a panel of experts in the field. Peer-reviewed journals, therefore, provide the reader with some support for the relevance and rigor of a study. Such studies are reviewed in terms of merit, clarity of research question, rigor in design of the study, data collection and analysis, and study implications. Keeping a literature search to only peer-reviewed journals is a good initial step to identifying information to help shape one's understanding of a given research question.

Literature reviews are used as a way to refine your question. Therefore, based on the current literature review about student athletes' adjustment to college, a potential refinement to the previous research question could be: "Do students involved in college sports have higher levels of college adjustment than regular students?" As shown, the question now includes the variables of interest—specifically, college sports and adjustment—and target population—in this case, college students (i.e., athletes, non-athletes).

Since the question now focuses on causation between variables, a best guess at what might be found once data is collected and analyzed might include the following:

— Are social networks more strongly related to college adjustment for student athletes than regular students?
— Do student athletes have better time management skills than regular students?
— Will student athletes report that social networks contributed to their college adjustment more or less than regular students?

Writing a literature review

Other ways to ensure organization in the literature search process include: taking notes, writing out a bibliography, and keeping it clean (alphabetical order, organized by topic). It is desirable to keep the articles you review organized, as these will serve as the references you cite when writing your literature review. It is recommended to download an electronic copy of a relevant article and save it in an appropriately labeled folder on an external/internal hard drive for future use. Another strategy that some of my students have shared is that they have kept their literature reviews using one of the qualitative software packages like N-Vivo or Atlas. Both packages allow you to store the articles and have each of the articles coded by the key words, phrases, or themes that you identify. The software will also link whatever direct quotes you identify and store with the respective article and author(s). It is important to ensure that all direct quotes are cited appropriately (we do not want to plagiarize). According to APA publication guidelines, paraphrasing is a way of using someone else's ideas but using your own words. This needs to be referenced without a specific page number, whereas direct quotes should be used sparingly and do need specific page references. Both of these methods can be catalogued through the respective software. This will make referencing easier when you are ready to write your own literature review.

It is important to understand that the literature search is not just an academic exercise to gather articles, but is a useful tool to help develop an argument that you will eventually collect data to help tell a story that addresses a problem. The process of the literature search will be the foundation for the development of a literature review. A literature review is defined as the way you will introduce a reader to a relevant and substantive research issue that has yet to be fully addressed and that you will be addressing through your study. The literature review justifies the need for a study by identifying, reviewing, and synthesizing the existing body of research on a given topic. You should include relevant information that addresses aspects of theory and other research studies that have focused on your research question.

Among other things, the aim of the literature review is to:

1. Introduce the reader to the problem of interest (e.g., student dropout, coping with divorce, promoting students' academic achievement, etc.).
2. Present, review, and synthesize previous research to provide the reader a background on the importance of the topic and where current thinking in the area is today.

3. Identify gaps in the literature and use this to build a case for one's study.
4. Identify the theory/theories that you are using to help define your research problem.
5. Specify the relationships between variables (hypothesis) that will guide the present study.

Hart (1999) indicates that the literature review should:

- distinguish what has been done before from what needs to be done
- discover important variables relevant to the topic
- synthesize and gain a new perspective
- identify relationships between ideas and practices
- establish the context of the topic or problem
- rationalize the significance of the problem
- enhance and acquire the subject vocabulary
- understand the structure of the subject
- relate ideas and theory to applications
- identify the main methodologies and research techniques that have been used
- place the research in a historical context to show familiarity with state-of-the-art developments (p. 27).

Creswell (1994) indicates that literature reviews should:

- present results of similar studies
- relate the present study to the ongoing dialogue in the literature
- provide a framework for comparing the results of a study with other studies

Similarly, Strike and Posner (1983) suggest that a literature review contain three characteristics:

- clarifies the problems within an area of study
- sheds light on the problems in the area by explaining strengths and limitations and indicating ways in which to address potential problems
- supports the notion of a good theory

The following page is a guide to help you organize your literature search based upon your research question.

LITERATURE SEARCH

State your question _____

_____

List questions you hope are already answered by previous research.

Likely sources where articles may be found.

Key Words

_____   _____   _____

_____   _____   _____

_____   _____   _____

_____   _____   _____

_____   _____   _____

_____   _____   _____

List relevant theories or models.

List authors, source, and date of relevant articles.

_____   _____

_____   _____

_____   _____

_____   _____

_____   _____

Other background information you could use.

Identify authors and articles.

_____

_____

_____

_____

_____

_____

List relevant theories or models.

List authors, source, and date of relevant articles.

_____

_____

_____

_____

_____

_____

_____

_____

_____

_____

Other background information you could use.

Identify authors and articles.

_____

_____

_____

_____

_____

_____

Identify race, gender, class biases from the literature.

List sources of information.

_____

_____

_____

_____

_____

_____

List other sources that may be relevant to your question.

Hypotheses

Up to this point, the focus has been on developing a question and how to conduct a literature search. There have been references to the variables that are being identified in your question. Remember, there are four types of questions: descriptive, relational, causal, and interactional. The first type, descriptive, is just describing the variables, and there is no relationship between them. The second type of question, relational, senses that there is a relationship, but it is unclear just what that relationship is. Therefore, these two types of questions would most likely be exploratory research, and there would NOT be a hypothesis generated. These studies would most likely be qualitative.

However, the causal and interactional questions would most likely generate some type of hypothesis. Thus, one of the things that you hope the literature review suggests would be to gain an understanding of the state of affairs regarding how the variables are related in your topic and the ways in which research has been conducted to answer the question. Only after a complete understanding of the research question and direction of the relationship between relevant variables can a research hypothesis be stated.

A hypothesis (discussed in more detail in chapter 7) can be defined as one's best educated guess about study findings. It is specified before conducting a study and provides the framework for the recruitment of study participants, collecting and analyzing data, as well as interpreting and reporting study findings. More specifically, the hypothesis can be described as a statement that characterizes the relationship between two or more variables, typically the independent and dependent variables. The hypothesis should only be stated after a complete review of the existing literature. There may be times when a question will not generate any causal relationships. This is most likely when the study is exploratory and your study is trying to determine if there is a relationship or not. These types of questions would be qualitative research questions.

Justification of the Study

As previously stated, there is a difference between hypothesis-testing research and decision-making research. To be able to understand which type of research you might be proposing, it is important to be able to justify your study as to who cares besides yourself. Granted, you are conducting the study because it is of interest to you, but is it of interest to anyone else or the field, and how is it of interest to them? These are important considerations as the field is requesting more information on accountability or the efficacy of the method that is being tested. Therefore, the task of answering (a) who cares, (b) what is the relevance, (c) how important is the correct answer, and (d) what are the implications of alternatives? is important prior to fully undertaking the task of a research study. In addition, as funding moves more toward providing services, these questions become important in demonstrating a link between research and practice.

Who cares?

These questions were very important in conducting the study about homeless shelters. It was very easy for the community to commit to building more shelter beds without looking at what happens in a shelter to address the problem. The community had an immediate problem and wanted an immediate solution. Conducting a study would delay a solution to the problem. Therefore, the answers to these questions had to be thought out very carefully before the commitment of resources to just build more shelter beds. The "Who Cares?" question then focused on a combination of people. Of course, there were the homeless people, but "who" also involved administrators of existing shelters as well as community leaders. The more inclusive you can be in identifying the "who" with an explanation of their role in the project, the greater the potential of building support and allies for the project. A general rule of thumb that I subscribe to is, "If one person plans a program, you are only guaranteed to have one person show up." Therefore, it is better to err on the side of inclusion.

Relevance to who cares?

Once the "who" has been identified, it is important to answer the other questions in relationship to the "who." For example, although the goal of the study of homeless shelters was the same—to identify what happens in a homeless shelter to address the problems of people who were homeless—the relevance of that goal is different for each population group. For homeless people, the relevance is to identify an appropriate service delivery system that would address their needs. Shelter professionals would see it as a way of informing the community of the types of services they provide to enhance potential funding to continue those services. Community leaders would want that information to assist in establishing criteria for who receives funding for what aspect of the program as well as being able to develop accountability standards to see how well the program is addressing those needs.

Do I need the right answer?

The answers to these questions relate to the needs of the people who want to be informed about the problem/question that led to the study. Thus, this is not testing a specific guess but looking at efficacy of services to assist in decision-making.

Alternative answers and their implications

It may be important to also identify some alternative answers based upon who cares about the study and what the specific interests are. Considering the sources and the implications of who cares may be helpful in the long run for urging people to support your position. For example, the drive for building more homeless shelters originated from the business community, which was interested in not having homeless persons sleeping on their doorsteps overnight, as there was a fear that it would drive away potential customers. Thus, by understanding their needs and desires, it was possible to not only understand the driving force behind building shelters, but also to work with the business community to develop appropriate alternatives so that their needs were met as well.

On the next page, answer the four questions and then use the answers to write a paragraph to support why you want to conduct this study.

JUSTIFYING THE STUDY

Answer each question, but first state your research question:

_____

(1)   Identify all sources who care about the answer.

_____

_____

_____

(2)   Describe the relevance for each source.

_____

_____

_____

(3)   Describe the importance of having the right answer for each source.

_____

_____

_____

(4)   Describe the implications of various possible answers for each source.

_____

_____

_____

(5) Write a paragraph justifying your study. Consider the questions above but feel free to modify or add to them.

_____

_____

_____

_____

_____

_____

(6) Describe whether your project is about testing hypotheses or can be used to assist in measuring the efficacy of a service.

_____

_____

Variables

U p to this point, you have been identifying concepts that relate to your research question. However, those concepts were somewhat abstract. Through the literature review, you should have begun to obtain some definition to those concepts. At this time, it is important for you to begin to define these concepts in some measurable way. This process is called **operationalizing**. When you operationalize a concept, you not only define it in measurable terms, but you change the concept into a variable.

There may be three types of variables that relate to your question. First, there are those variables that are independent variables. These variables stand on their own merit and may be presumed as causal variables. Second, there are the dependent variables. Dependent variables are the outcomes of the interaction of the independent variables or the presumed effect from the causal variable. Thinking back to the cake analogy in the first chapter, the cake is the dependent variable of the interaction of the independent variables, which are the raw ingredients. Finally, there are control variables. These are factors that you want to maintain as constant so you can obtain a true picture of the cause-and-effect relationship between independent and dependent variables.

Thus, in reflecting back to the analogy of baking a cake from the first chapter, the raw ingredients are your independent variables. The dependent variable is the cake. The control variables become the oven temperature, the size of the pan, the altitude, and length of mixing time. These are all factors that you control in determining the effect of the independent variables on the dependent variable.

It is not always as easy to determine independent, dependent, and control variables in a research study. There is the potential for a tremendous amount of variance in terms, and much relies on how you operationalize the concepts. For example, in the study of homeless shelters, an assumption existed that people with minimal support systems had a greater likelihood of being homeless; thus, if the shelter created support mechanisms, then there would a mechanism for addressing the problems that led the person to become homeless. This led to the independent variable of identifying types of social supports, and the dependent variable became resolving the problems that led to homelessness. Social supports could be broken into formal social supports (linkage to the formal support system established to address the problems) and informal social supports (interaction with friends and family members). The control variables became limiting the sample to single adult males rather than the entire spectrum of the homeless population. This then also led to another control variable being the nature of the shelters being used in the study, or adult male, 24-hour, emergency shelters. Thus, by operationalizing the definitions in this manner, it is possible to create variables that can be tested. However, this excludes other factors that may be contributing factors to being homeless, such as substance abuse, mental health factors, or even adverse childhood experiences (ACEs). Thus, operationalizing variables becomes a limiting factor to a study.

Therefore, not only does operationalizing variables limit the study into identifiable ways to measure the outcomes, but it also addresses some of the researcher's bias in what is being studied. This becomes something that needs to be addressed as one of the limitations to the study at some point in time. Describing limitations to your study will be more fully discussed in chapter 13. On the other hand, operationalizing variables helps to identify the causal relationship that is being tested between the variables. The difficulty arises in operationalizing the concepts. When there is just not enough information about the concepts in a particular setting to identify specific operational definitions, one may be relegated to exploratory research to create operational definitions or a preliminary or pilot study that will help to identify the variables. Some may classify this as an exploratory sequential design mixed method study (Creswell, 2015, pg. 41), or one where qualitative data collection and analysis is used to build a quantitative study. This lack of operational definitions leads to a qualitative research design. That will be discussed later. However, this is mentioned to demonstrate that in most hypothesis-testing research questions, there is an ability to identify variables that relate to the problems that arise, and operationalizing creates a way to measure those variables. For example, both formal and informal social supports could be defined by linkages and contacts, but how does someone describe the quality of that interaction? On the following page, identify your variables from your research question and define them in measurable terms.

VARIABLES AND DEFINITIONS

Identify the independent, dependent, and control variables in your question. Dependent variables are those which your study seeks to explain or understand. Independent variables are those which you expect may have an effect on the dependent variables. Control variables are included to enhance the validity of the design by eliminating rival explanations or specifying the conditions under which something occurs.

For each variable, provide an operational definition reflecting how this variable will be observed in this study.

Dependent variable(s)	Operational Definition

homeless person   Single adult who does not have a place to live and has not had a permanent residence for at least three months.

Independent variables	Operational Definition

Homeless shelter   24-hour emergency facility providing room and board and services to homeless people.

Control variable(s)	Operational Definition

single adults   Single adults without any dependents coming to the shelter with them.

Greater Bridgeport area   Shelters in the Bridgeport-Fairfield area in Connecticut.

VARIABLES AND DEFINITIONS

Identify the independent, dependent, and control variables in your question. Dependent variables are those which your study seeks to explain or understand. Independent variables are those which you expect may have an effect on the dependent variables. Control variables are included to enhance the validity of the design by eliminating rival explanations or specifying the conditions under which something occurs.

For each variable, provide an operational definition reflecting how this variable will be observed in this study.

Dependent variable(s)   Operational Definition

_____   _____

_____   _____

_____   _____

Independent variables   Operational Definition

_____   _____

_____   _____

_____   _____

_____   _____

Control variable(s)   Operational Definition

_____   _____

_____   _____

_____   _____

_____   _____

Research by Numbers: Descriptive Statistics

O nce you have identified and defined your variables, it is important to describe them. This is called descriptive statistics and begins the process of gathering and analyzing data for the purpose of describing the characteristics of the data. Descriptive statistics only describe the characteristics of the data. No inferences can be made from this type of data.

It is important to understand that there are two branches of statistics: descriptive and inferential. Descriptive statistics deals with using statistics, such as frequency distributions and measures of central tendency/variability, to understand or describe characteristics of a group in which data has been obtained or collected. This can include, for example, the average test performance of a classroom or school or the number of clients served at a clinic over a two-week period.

Inferential statistics, on the other hand, are statistical tests where variables are analyzed in relationship to other variables with an understanding to see how one relates to the other (discussed in more detail in chapter 10). From these types of statistical tests, it is possible to make inferences about how these interactions might relate to the larger, target population. For example, assigning a group of persons to one-on-one counseling for substance abuse while comparing the effects of another group to traditional group interventions for substance abusers and then assessing the sobriety levels of each group would demonstrate the use of inferential statistics. In this case, if participants exposed to group treatment reported higher levels of sobriety than one-on-one counseling, then it suggests that group treatment may be more effective than individual therapy. Remember that these types of studies do not prove one form is better than another but only suggest it in this particular instance. A meta-analysis of a number of studies would need to be done to truly demonstrate evidence that one type is better than another. More on inferential statistics in a later chapter. This section will provide an overview of descriptive statistics in social science research.

Levels of Measurement

In general, research questions situated in the social sciences are based on understanding the characteristics of or relationships between variables, such as: motivation, leadership, academic achievement, adjustment, etc. Consider the following research question: "Does participation in an after-school program promote third-grade students' academic achievement?" As stated, this is a non-directional hypothesis that can be formally tested. It includes the independent variable of after-school program and dependent variable of academic achievement. The target population is third-grade students.

In this example, formal hypothesis testing requires collecting data to determine whether those who participate in the after-school program do obtain higher achievement scores than those who do not participate. Say the data (on one-hundred students: fifty students enrolled in program, fifty not enrolled in program) we collect includes whether or not the student participated in the program and academic achievement scores, as measured through a standardized measure of academic achievement.

Prior to conducting an appropriate statistical analysis to answer our question, we must first have an understanding of how the variables are measured. This will allow us to select the most appropriate analysis to determine whether those enrolled in the program do in fact obtain higher achievement scores than those not enrolled.

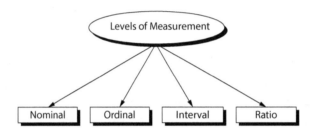

FIGURE 6.1 LEVELS OF MEASUREMENT

As indicated in figure 6.1 above, there are four levels of measurement for categorizing variables. These include: nominal, ordinal, interval, and ratio. Categorization of a variable into one of the four categories is based on how it is measured. For example, the number of days absent can be measured in a number of ways. For example, we may ask a student to estimate the number of days absent by providing a specific number. Here, the student could say they have missed twelve days of school this past year. On the other hand, the variable absence could be measured by having the student circle the category that represents number of school days missed, such as: 0–5, 6–10, 11–15, and so on.

In the former case, absence was measured as a continuous variable (days absent could range from 0 to 100+ days); in the latter, absences were measured as a categorical variable (days absent based on selected category—0–5, 6–10, etc.). Based on these diverse approaches to measuring the variable "absence," we can identify its corresponding level of measurement.

At the lowest level, a nominal variable is one that corresponds to measuring something based on its group membership, such as gender, race/ethnicity, program area, car brand, etc. Therefore, any qualitative-type variable (gender, religion, immigration status, etc.) is on a nominal level of measurement—that is, membership to a particular group does not suggest any type of ranking or one group possessing more of an attribute than the other.

Instances in which a variable takes on the distinct property of rank-ordering individuals (or objects) can then be categorized as possessing an ordinal level of measurement. Examples of ordinal variables include: position in marathon (e.g., first, second, third, etc.), grade level, and classification of achievement based on test scores (e.g., below average, average, above average). The shared characteristic of this variable set is that they not only indicate one's group membership, but that one's classification indicates a higher level of possession of the measured trait—such as speed, amount of education, and amount of academic achievement.

Noticeably, it is unknown of the distance between the different values of the variable. For the variable speed (as measured by one's standing in a marathon race), for example, we only know what position each runner was placed (first, second, third, fourth, etc.). We do not, however, know the distance between each runner's position, such as the number of seconds/minutes that separated the first- and second-place runners.

This leads to variables categorized on an interval level of measurement. If, in the previous example, we knew the actual time associated with each runner's position in a race and used this to measure the variable speed, it would be on an interval level of measurement. That is, if the first-place runner's time was three hours and fifteen minutes, and the second-place runner's time was three hours and thirty minutes, we can determine that the number of minutes between the runner's times was fifteen. Likewise, any variable measured in terms of a total score or time (seconds, minutes, etc.) is on an interval level of measurement. Thus, if we measured the variables academic achievement, depression, anxiety, and motivation using some sort of standardized test or self-administered questionnaire and used obtained scores to represent one's standing (low, middle, high) on the trait, the variables would be on an interval level of measurement. Interval variables possess the characteristics of nominal and ordinal variables but also include the property of recognizing the distance between variable values. As another example, we know a student who obtained a score of ninety on a test scored ten points higher than another student with a score of eighty, who in turn scored ten points higher than a student with a score of seventy.

The ratio level of measurement is the fourth category. Variables on a ratio level of measurement have the properties of the aforementioned types but possess the property of having an absolute value of zero. For example, if the variable "time spent reading" was measured by the number of minutes spent reading, it would be on a ratio level of measurement. Specifically, we could objectively assign a student a score of zero if they never picked up the book (no time spent reading) or assign a value of forty-five minutes to another student who read for this amount of time. Even though someone could obtain a score of zero on a particular test, test scores are interval variables. In this instance, a score of zero does not indicate zero intelligence or academic achievement; rather, it indicates that the test may have been too difficult and re-administration of an alternative test may yield a different score (perhaps a score of two out of ten on a spelling quiz).

Therefore, it is critical to consider the level of measurement of the variables of interest to help you in determining how they can be used to address your research question.

The basic difference between interval and ratio data is that ratio data has an absolute zero score. Some statistical software packages, such as SPSS, do not make a distinction between interval and ratio data but classify it as continuous data.

Test your understanding by considering the variables listed below to identify their level of measurement.

- Gender
- Grade level (first, second, etc.)
- Intelligence test scores (e.g., 75, 89, 110)
- Temperature (e.g., -15, 0, 5, 32, 75)
- Years of social work experience
- Religion
- Social security number
- Time reading book
- Response options (e.g., always, sometimes, never)
- GRE scores

Visual tools to present the characteristics of the data collected can be powerful ways for presenting the information to address the driving research question. For example, if data was collected on a sample of one-hundred clients receiving rehabilitative counseling, one may be interested in knowing the number of males and females, the average age of the clients, as well as the number of years receiving clinical services, among others.

Frequency distributions provide a useful approach for understanding characteristics of a variable in which data was obtained. In particular, graphs provide a way of looking at the distributions of your variables and, thus, make use of an exploratory data-analysis approach to understanding the characteristics of your sample in relation to that variable (e.g., motivation, sex, race/ethnicity, etc.).

Graphs

We can define a distribution as the arrangement of a set of values for a variable in order of group membership (racial/ethnic group, sex, car brand, etc.) or magnitude (income, grade level, etc.). The three most commonly used frequency distributions that will be covered here include the bar chart, histogram, and frequency polygon. Each provides a graphical depiction of the standing of individuals on that variable—such as number of males/females or number of students associated with program areas (higher ed., special education, counseling, etc.).

Figure Bar Graphs

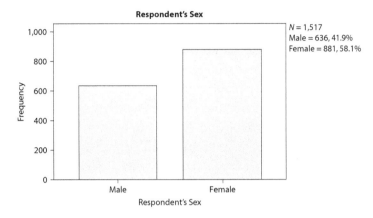

FIGURE 6.2 BAR GRAPHS

The first frequency distribution we consider is the bar chart. As shown, a bar chart is a simple representation of the number (or percentage) of individuals belonging to each category of a variable. Based on the information presented in this bar chart, we see that there are 636 males and 881 females. When reviewing the distributions of variables in graphs, the horizontal line (called the x-axis) is used to indicate the different values of a variable; the vertical axis (called the y-axis) indicates the units (frequency/count, percentage) to indicate the number of individuals falling within each category of the variable. Bar charts are used to examine the distributions of variables on a nominal (race/ethnicity, job) or ordinal (educational level, grade level, etc.) level of measurement. As you can see from the figure above, the bars are distinct from each other and do not touch.

Figure Histograms

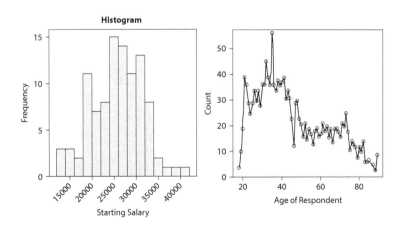

FIGURE 6.3 HISTOGRAMS

Histograms represent another way to look at the distributions of continuous variables or those variables on an interval or ratio level of measurement. Specifically, a histogram is a graphical representation of a frequency distribution where the frequency corresponding to each score level is shown by the height of a rectangle bar above the score, which shows all values represented in the graph. Thus, histograms serve particularly useful to summarize information in a large data, say when data is collected on 1,000 students and it is desired to see how spread out the scores are.

Unlike bar charts that report the number of individuals belonging to a specific variable value, histograms summarize continuous data, and as such, the bars are connected to demonstrate the relationship between the categories. Development of histograms follow a three-step process summarized here. First, the data is divided into classes of equal intervals. For example, say you have achievement data collected on one-hundred twelfth-grade students, and scores on the achievement scale indicate the total number of items correct out of one hundred—so scores can range between zero and one hundred. In this case, perhaps you group the data into equal intervals of five, so that the first bar corresponds to scores ranging from 0–5, the second bar for scores 6–10, and the third 11–15, and so on.

The next step then involves counting the number of observations with values falling into each of the categories. Say there are four students in the sample of one hundred with scores that fall within the range of 0–5, and two with scores from 6–10. The last step is creating the histogram graph by using bars to indicate the number of observations falling within each score range (e.g., 0–5, 6–10, 11–15, etc.).

The above histogram shows the distribution of values for the variable "starting salary." Based on the presented information, we can see salaries range from somewhere around $13,000/year to more than $40,000, with the majority of values falling around $25,000. Also, we can see that there are very few individuals with starting salaries above $30,000.

Figure Frequency Polygon

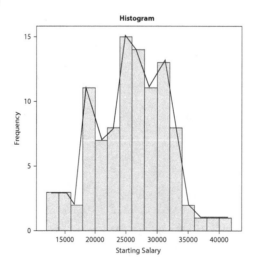

FIGURE 6.4A FREQUENCY POLYGON

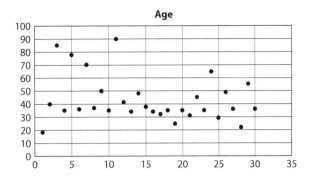

FIGURE 6.4B FREQUENCY POLYGON AGES OF RESPONDENTS

Ages of Respondents

Frequency polygons represent a frequency distribution not in terms of bars, but by a line connecting the total number of individuals (or objects) within each category. As displayed on the first figure above, the red line would be used to depict the distribution of the variable "starting salary," as opposed to the bars used for the histogram. Thus, the frequency polygon yields the same information about the distribution of a variable as a histogram, just in a different style using a line instead of rectangular bars.

The second frequency polygon figure displays the distribution for the variable "age." As shown, ages are displayed along the x-axis, with the number (count) along the y-axis. The graph indicates that the ages of individuals from whom data was collected range from about eighteen to ninety years, with most individuals in the sample being around thirty-five years of age. Also, the majority of individuals in the sample are less than forty years old, with lower numbers of individuals in the upper age groups. This frequency polygon only lists the scatter plot of the items, and from the scatter plot, it is possible to gain an understanding of how the line would appear. If we were to draw a line, then it would run through the mean or average of each age depicted on the chart.

When looking at distributions, one factor to consider is whether there is one value of a variable occurring most frequently in the distribution or whether two values are equally represented. When one value occurs most frequently within a distribution, resulting in a single peak in the distribution, the distribution can be characterized as unimodal, as depicted in the above frequency distribution.

Characteristics of Distribution

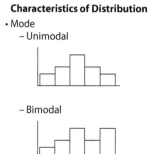

FIGURE 6.5 CHARACTERISTICS OF DISTRIBUTION

Characteristics of Distribution

On the other hand, when two values occur at about the same frequency, the distribution will have two peaks and is referred to as bimodal, as depicted by the picture labeled bimodal distribution.

Another characteristic to consider when inspecting a variable's distribution is whether it is skewed. That is, are the values centered, concentrated at the high end, or concentrated at the low end? As you may be familiar, this deals with whether a distribution is normal, positively skewed, or negatively skewed.

A normal distribution is one in which the values of a variable fall around a center value, with fewer observations at the lower or upper end of the distribution, as depicted by this diagram.

Standard Deviation

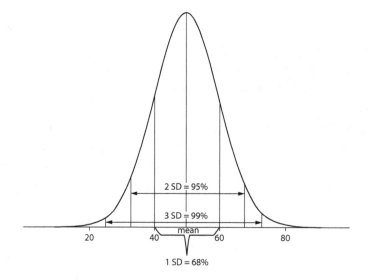

FIGURE 6.6 STANDARD DEVIATION

As you can see, there is equal distribution on either side of the midpoint. It is also important to understand issues of standard deviation, as that will relate to probability later. From the diagram, one standard deviation is the most concentrated part of the population and represents 68 percent of the population. Two standard deviations reflect 95 percent of the population. And three standard deviations represent 99 percent of the population. Thus, when you are looking at whether an intervention occurred based on chance or by the intervention, if the statistical test can demonstrate that the effect of the intervention resulted in change of three standard deviations or 99 percent of the population, then there is a .01 probability (or 99 times out of 100). The standard is to have a .05 probability or better, which translates as two standard deviations (or 95 times out of 100).

However, populations do not always fall within a normal distribution and can be either negatively or positively skewed. These concepts are not always intuitive to how they sound, though. A negatively skewed distribution occurs when the majority of the observations are toward the high end (right side) of the distribution, with fewer values falling at the low end. An illustration of a negatively skewed distribution is shown here.

Negative Skew

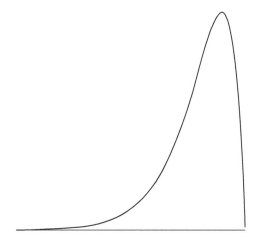

FIGURE 6.7 NEGATIVE SKEW

Contrary, a positively skewed distribution has values located predominantly at the lower end of the distribution (left side) and fewer observations at the upper end. The distribution of a variable is labeled according to the direction in which the tail points—the negative or positive end of the distribution.

Immediately below are two variables, one for the "highest year of school completed," and the second is "number of brothers and sisters." For the variable education level, the lowest year is zero and the highest is twenty years, and it is a unimodal distribution. Overall, it is roughly normally distributed with the appearance of one outlier, the value of zero. An outlier is any value or score that deviates strongly from the other values in the distribution.

Positive Skew

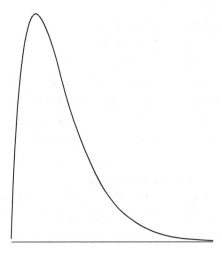

FIGURE 6.8 POSITIVE SKEW

The second histogram depicts the distribution for the variable of "number of brothers and sisters." This is a good example of a positively skewed distribution that is unimodal, with the majority of values falling at the lower end of the distribution and fewer at the upper end. The range is zero to twenty-six, which looks like an outlier, along the values around eighteen and twenty-two. Thus, only until you visually inspect the distribution of a variable can you determine its characteristics—that is, whether it is normally distributed (or skewed), unimodal/bimodal, range (low and high value), and the presence of outliers.

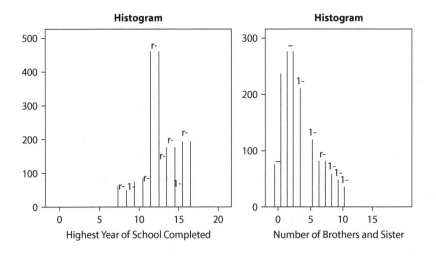

FIGURE 6.9 POPULATION DISTRIBUTION HISTOGRAMS

As discussed, distributions play an important role in understanding information on the individuals from which data were collected. Upon data collection, it is desirable to know a bit about the sample, such as the number of males and females, race/ethnic groups, and age. Frequency distributions serve as one method to understand the data. The three types of distributions discussed here included: bar chart, histogram, and frequency polygon.

Regardless of which frequency distribution is used, consideration of the distribution's shape (or level of skewness), modality (unimodal, bimodal), range, and outliers will aid in understanding the variable.

Now that understanding population distribution has been explained, it is important to introduce the statistical tests that are associated with descriptive statistics. In particular, within this section we will discuss the estimation and use of measures of central tendency and variability. Just a word of caution: descriptive statistics describe the population and do not predict. Thus, the statistics introduced will be those that help to describe the characteristics of the population being studied.

Measures of Central Tendency

Measures of central tendency are used across practice and research to summarize information collected on a group of individuals or objects. Measures of central tendency include the mean, median, and mode. Collectively, these measures indicate the value in which values of a variable fall. The **mean** is the **average** value in a set of scores, or those variables on an interval or ratio level of measurement. Two examples include (a) using scores on a measure of client empowerment following participation in a job training program, and (b) determining the average test performance of one classroom or grade level. The **mode** is the **most frequently occurring** score in a distribution. Last, the **median** is the **central score in a distribution**. We will discuss each in detail.

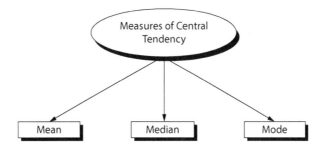

FIGURE 6.10 MEASURES OF CENTRAL TENDENCY

Mean

The mean is the average score in a distribution. The mean is estimated by adding the scores in a distribution and then dividing by the total number of observations. Thus, to calculate the mean, you need to have all the scores in the distribution and knowledge of the total number of individuals from which the data were collected. The mean is used for variables on an interval and ratio level of measurement, such as survey/test scores or time spent reading. One cannot use a mean for nominal or ordinal data.

Estimating Mean

An example for calculating the mean is provided here, based on the following four scores: 99, 88, 94, and 100. Thus, the mean is obtained by adding the scores to get 381 and then dividing by four to get our mean of 95.25. In social science research, the mean is most commonly used to summarize the scores of groups of individuals; for example, comparing average scores between two groups or comparing scores between different times. In clinical settings, the mean is used in a similar manner—to determine clients' satisfaction with therapy or judge quality of life or some other personal trait prior to, during, or after some therapeutic intervention.

Median

The median represents the middle score in a distribution. Calculation of the median requires first sorting the values in a distribution in ascending order and then counting from either end to find the middle score. Here, the median for these scores of 99, 80, 78, 76, 74, 41, 40, and 40 is 75—obtained by counting four in from the top and bottom. Thus, because four from the top gives us 76 and from the bottom 74, we take the average of these values to obtain 75, the median. If the score of 40 only occurred once, the median value would be 76. Thus, each score is counted in the estimation of the median, regardless of the number of times it occurs in the distribution.

The median is used as the measure of central tendency for variables on ordinal, interval, and ratio level of measurement.

Mode

The third, and final, measure of central tendency is the mode, defined as the most frequently occurring observation in the distribution. Unlike the previous measures of central tendency, the mode can be used for both qualitative (sex, race/ethnicity, religion) and quantitative (test scores) variables. In the example of these numbers, 3, 4, 7, 8, 9, 7, 4, 7, 10, 2, 7, 1, the mode is 7, which occurs three times in this score set. Thus, the mode is appropriate to indicate the most frequently occurring value in a distribution for variables on a nominal, ordinal, interval, and ratio level of measurement.

Identifying the Mode

In the previous example that looked at frequency distributions for the variables "starting salary" and "age," both are unimodal distributions. Whereas the "salary" distribution is roughly normal, the "age" distribution is positively skewed. The mode of "salary" corresponds to the bar for $25,000; the mode for "age" is roughly thirty-five years of age.

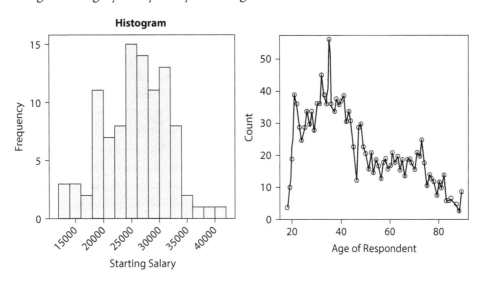

FIGURE 6.11 FREQUENCY DISTRIBUTION SALARY & AGE

Central Tendencies in Distributions

Here, we have examples of the three previously discussed skewed distributions: normal (no skewness), negatively skewed, and positively skewed. Within a normal distribution, all three measures of central tendency are the same. That is, they occur at the center of the distribution. Within a negatively skewed distribution, the mode is located on the hump, or where the most frequently occurring score is located. The mean, however, is pulled toward the lower end, or tail, of the distribution. It is pulled to the tail of the distribution because outliers and extreme values affect the mean. The median, on the other hand, is located at the place in the distribution that balances the distribution. That is, if you were to balance the distribution on a triangle, the location that equals out the two sides is the median. Thus, in the presence of skewed distributions (positive or negative), the median is the desired measure of central tendency.

Similarly, in the instance of a positively skewed distribution, the mode occurs at the most frequently occurring score, located at the higher end of the distribution. The mean, since it is influenced by extreme scores at either end of the distribution, is pulled up. Again, the median is located at the place in the distribution that balances it out if you were to put it on a triangle.

Normal Distribution

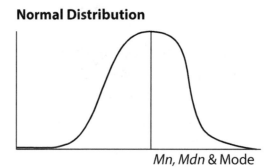

Mn, Mdn & Mode

▶ **Negatively Skewed Distribution**

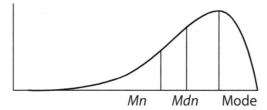

Mn   Mdn   Mode

▶ **Positively Skewed Distribution**

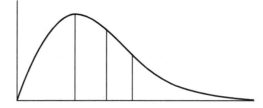

FIGURE 6.12 CENTRAL TENDENCIES IN DISTRIBUTION

Measures of Variability

Measures of central tendency provide a useful way to summarize the values in a distribution. That is, they provide an indication of what value in the distribution that other values fall around. Just as important is characterizing the spread of your values in the distribution, based on measures of variability. These include the variance, standard deviation, and range. Each possesses unique properties that make it a useful index to judge whether a score set is homogeneous or heterogeneous in nature.

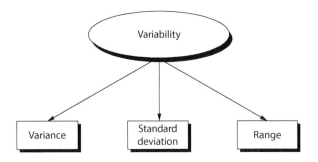

FIGURE 6.13 VARIABILITY

Tabled Data

To promote our understanding of the use of measures of variability to characterize the spread of scores in a distribution, consider this table. Here, we have data collected on ten individuals (listed in rows) on variables x (Column 2) and y (Column 5). We can say that Measures X and Y are spelling (Variable X) and reading fluency (Variable Y), for example. As shown, Student 1 obtained a score of 10 on Measure X and a score of 18 on Measure Y. Likewise, Student 2 also scored a 10 on Measure X and a 16 on Measure Y, whereas Student 10 obtained a score of 1 on both Measures X and Y.

Student	x	$(x - \bar{x})$	$(x - \bar{x})^2$	y	$(y - \bar{y})$	$(y - \bar{y})^2$	$(x - \bar{x})(y - \bar{y})$
1	10	4	16	18	8	64	32
2	10	4	16	16	6	36	24
3	9	3	9	18	8	64	24
4	7	1	1	12	2	4	2
5	6	0	0	10	0	0	0
6	5	−1	1	9	−1	1	1
7	5	−1	1	9	−1	1	1
8	4	−2	4	4	−6	36	12
9	3	−3	9	3	−7	49	21
10	1	−5	25	1	−9	81	45
	Σx = 60	Σ = 0	Σ = 82	Σy = 100	Σ = 0	Σ = 336	Σ = 162

Mean of Test X: 60/10 = 6   Mean of Test Y: 100/10 = 10
Median of Test X: 5.5   Median of Test Y: 9.5
Mode of Test X: 10, 5   Mode of Test Y: 18, 9

FIGURE 6.14 TABLE OF TEN STUDENT SCORES

As shown on the bottom of the slide, the mean of Measure X is 6, whereas the mean for Measure Y is 10. The median for Measures X and Y are 5.5 and 9.5, respectively. Both measures are bimodal with the modes of Measure X being 5 and 10; the modes of Measure Y are 9 and 18.

Variability

Here, we are provided the equation for calculating the variance, a measure of variability, indicating the spread of scores. As shown, calculation of the variance requires several values, including: the sum of each individual's score in the distribution (symbolized as x subscript i) minus the mean (or average score of distribution), and divided by the sample size (used in denominator, symbolized as n).

$$\sigma^2 = \frac{\Sigma(x_i - \bar{x})^2}{n}$$

$$\sigma_x^2 = \frac{82}{10} = 8.2$$

$$\sigma_y^2 = \frac{336}{10} = 33.6$$

FIGURE 6.15 VARIANCE

In order to fully understand the estimation of the variance, let's use the previous dataset as a basis to understand the variance. Let's first consider the numerator, where the first step is subtracting the mean from each individual score in the distribution. So, let's refer back to the third column in the table. Here, then, we see the deviation score for each individual in the distribution when we subtract the mean from individual scores. For example, Student 1's deviation score is 4, obtained by subtracting the mean of 6 from 10. Likewise, subtracting the mean of 6 from Student 3's score of 9 yields a deviation score of 3. This is the first requirement of estimating the variance—subtracting the mean from each score.

Inspection of the equation now requires us to square each deviation score. We do this because to determine the variance, we will need to add up all the scores and divide by n, indicating that the variance is an average—the average amount of spread of the scores around the mean. However, if we simply added up the deviation scores without squaring, it would come out to zero. This is because half the scores fall above the mean and half below the mean. Therefore, we square the deviation scores to eliminate the negative values. This is what we see in Column 4 of the table, the squared deviation value. Thus, if we square Student 1's deviation score of 4, we get 16.

Likewise squaring Student 6's deviation score of 1 yields a score of 1. Thus, the result of squaring each student's deviation score yields the values reported in Column 4. This satisfies most of the steps in the numerator, with one exception. That is, once we square each student's deviation score, we need to add them up, as indicated by the sigma symbol (Σ) in the numerator. By summing the values in Column 4, we obtain a value of 82, as provided in the last row of the column. This value of 82 is the numerator in the equation. The last step, as indicated by the equation, is to divide 82 by the total sample size, n, which is 10. Thus, 82 divided by 10 is 8.2, which is the variance. Apply the same steps to estimate the variance of Measure Y scores.

Typically, we do not rely on the variance to describe the spread of scores in a distribution. Instead, we routinely use the mean in conjunction with the standard deviation to characterize the spread of scores around the mean. Therefore, the standard deviation indicates the average spread of scores around the mean.

Standard Deviation

The meaning of standard deviation was graphically presented in Figure 6.6 when describing a normal distribution. Below are the formulas for calculating variance and standard deviation. Both are the same except for one small difference. To estimate the standard deviation requires taking the square root of the variance. The reason we take the square root of the variance is that to estimate the variance, we had to square the deviation scores of each individual in the distribution. If you recall, we did this to eliminate negative values. Because of this, the variance is not on the same scale as the mean. To obtain a measure of variability that is on the same scale as the mean, we use the standard deviation. Therefore, to estimate the standard deviation, the variance must first be calculated and then take the square root of it. Within our example, taking the square root of the variance from Measure X, we get 2.86. Therefore, now we have a measure of variability that is on the same scale as the mean of Measure X, which was 6. Whenever the mean is reported, so should be the standard deviation, as both provide critical information to interpret the information summarizing the data collected on a group of individuals.

Statistical packages for computers will provide you with the numbers for these factors. The calculations are shown here to provide you with an understanding of how the computer works to arrive at those numbers. The calculations are not being provided to scare you away from the research, but to empower you with the knowledge on how it is done.

Properties of Standard Deviation

Here are some general properties associated with the standard deviation. Because the standard deviation indicates the average amount of spread of the scores around the mean, it should always be reported along with the mean. Second, when all scores in a distribution are equal (or when everyone obtains the same score), the standard deviation will be zero, indicating no deviation of scores around the mean. Third, like the mean, the standard deviation (and variance for that matter) is affected by outliers, or extreme values at the high or low end of the distribution. Thus, outliers will give the appearance that scores are more spread out than they may be. This indicates the importance of using the frequency distributions, as previously discussed, to identify the presence of extreme scores in our distribution, because they will directly affect our measures of central tendency and variability.

Range

The last measure of variability is the range, which is simply the difference between the lowest and highest score in the distribution. Thus, for Measure X in our previous example, the range would be calculated by subtracting 1 (the lowest score in the distribution) from 10 (highest score in distribution) to obtain a value of 9—the range.

Descriptive Statistics—Applied Example

This illustrates the use of measures of central tendency and variability to tell a story on the non-cognitive self-perceptions of freshman college students across a host of measures. These measures include: motivation, metacognition, as well as whether they characterize themselves as deep or surface learners. The values of 1 and 2 following each variable in Column 1 correspond to whether the score refers to a pre-test or post-test. So, let's consider the information provided in the table. All scores are based on students' responses across a set of items with a Likert response scale—strongly disagree to strongly agree. Thus, scores can range from 1 (strongly disagree) to 5 (strongly agree).

	Central Tendency			Variability		
	Mean	Median	Mode	SD	Variance	Range
Meta.1	3.91	3.90	4.00	0.49	0.17	3.65
Meta.2	3.67	3.75	3.00	0.59	0.35	4.00
Mot.1	4.09	4.08	3.96	0.41	0.17	3.36
Mot.2	3.69	3.76	3.00	0.61	0.37	4.00
Deep 1	3.64	3.60	3.60	0.49	0.24	3.30
Deep 2	3.41	3.30	3.00	0.61	0.37	4.00
Surf.1	2.45	2.40	2.30	0.51	0.27	3.50
Surf.2	3.04	3.00	3.00	0.64	0.40	4.00

Note. N = 554. Meta = Metacognition, Mot. = Motivation, Deep = Deep Learner, Surf. = Surface Learner

FIGURE 6.16 DESCRIPTIVE STATISTICS—APPLIED EXAMPLE

The first row corresponds to students' perceived levels of metacognition in their studying, or the degree to which they review their work and make necessary corrections. The mean of 3.91 for Meta. 1 indicates that students generally "agreed" (since the value is close to the score of 4, or "agree") that they monitor and modify their learning and academic behavior. The median approximates the mean, indicating a symmetrical distribution. The mode indicates that a score of 4 was the most frequently occurring value in the distribution. The standard deviation of .49 (square root of the variance of .17) suggests that scores fluctuated about a half a point around the mean. The range indicates the difference between the lowest and highest average score was 3.65.

Based on measures obtained at Time 1, we can see that students had the highest scores for motivation, with a mean of 4.09. Students also reported being more deep learners than surface learners, with a mean of 3.64 compared to 2.45, respectively.

Now, let's see how their Time 1 scores compared to the same measures when obtained at Time 2, collected at the end of the freshman year. A comparison of Time 1 and Time 2 means indicates that students became less motivated, less metacognitively aware, less deep learners, and became more surface learners at Time 2. That is, all scores decreased, with the exception of their surface scores, which increased. Also, a review of the standard deviation indicates that the students' scores were more varied at Time 2, compared to Time 1. This is interesting and suggests that students had similar levels of motivation and metacognition at Time 1, but following one year in their undergraduate studies became less motivated and metacognitively engaged. They also became less involved in their learning, as indicated by drops in deep learning scores.

Although we cannot predict anything using descriptive statistics, there is much to be understood. We learn about a group of individuals where data were obtained just by examining the previously discussed descriptive statistics to suggest trends in the population. The question of population to study relates to issues of sampling that will be discussed in chapter 9. However, prior to deciding on the population to study to address your question, it is important to become clearer about the relationship between the variables that will be studied in order to make an informed decision about the proper sample to answer the research question(s). Thus, the next chapter will focus on hypotheses, or understanding the relationships between variables.

Hypotheses

To this point, we have identified a research question, how to conduct a literature search to gather more information and narrow our question, develop a rationale for studying the question, and how to graphically present the variables related to the question using descriptive statistics. However, we have not talked about the relationship between the variables and how one variable may influence another. When beginning to look at relationships between variables, we are really talking about hypotheses or hypothesis development.

Simply stated, a hypothesis is the probability statement about the relationship between variables, or in other words, how likely one variable will affect the other. By returning to the cake metaphor, when all the raw ingredients interact appropriately with each other while maintaining the controls for oven temperature, pan size, etc., then you will have a delicious cake. Therefore, the probability that the cake will be good each time is high as long as you follow the directions.

The probability of repetition in the social sciences is not as guaranteed as baking a cake, which is why there continues to be research questions about interactions between different variables. The literature review helps to suggest certain inferences about the relationship between the variables that we are about to test through the research question. It is these inferences, then, that lead to a hypothesis that will be tested through the research process.

As discussed, variables (e.g., client change) in research can be classified based on their relationship to other variables (e.g., therapeutic process). The independent variable is the variable believed to influence (e.g., specific therapy) the dependent variable (e.g., client system change). Technically, the independent variable is the manipulating variable—be it a specific intervention, therapeutic intervention. On the other hand, the dependent variable is the one that is being influenced by the independent variable—or the variable that depends on the other. Hence the cake example described in chapter 1.

Take, for example, the following hypothesis: enrollment in an after-school literacy program will improve third-grade English Language Learners' reading fluency. Here, the after-school literacy program is the independent variable, or the manipulating variable. Through student enrollment in the program, there is a potential change that is being sought. To measure change by this specific independent variable, then, a control might be to measure the change in individuals not enrolled in the program. The desired change or dependent variable is reading fluency. In other words, we are testing the programmatic effects of the after-school literacy program on improving reading fluency. A word of caution at this point in time is that this is not taking into account other factors that might be changing reading fluency, such as the group effect. More of this will be discussed in the next chapter when discussing research design.

Take another example: "Will cognitive behavioral therapy (CBT) assist returning soldiers' symptoms associated with post-traumatic stress disorder (PTSD)?" Here, the independent variable is CBT (the individual could receive either CBT or some other therapy type). The dependent variable is severity of symptoms associated with PTSD—such as depression, anxiety, etc. Again, based upon the design, the question is whether one is testing the effects of CBT on improving factors associated with PTSD independent of other therapeutic techniques or whether the research design will test CBT in relationship to other therapeutic techniques.

Thus, in thinking about hypothesis development in empirical research, there are five general roles that the hypothesis takes:

1. Brings together information to enable the researcher to make a tentative statement about how the variables in the study are related.
2. Stimulates a research endeavor that results in accumulation of new knowledge.
3. Provides a testable statement in a research study.
4. Frames the research.
5. Provides a framework for reporting the findings and conclusions of the study.

From these statements, you can see that hypothesis development relates with causal and inter-actional types of questions, which relates more to quantitative types of research methods. It is still important to understand that if your question is asking to describe a situation or to understand how two or more variables relate to each other, these empirical questions are more exploratory and would necessitate using qualitative measures to arrive at an answer. As described below, a relational question would be a non-directional hypothesis since it is exploring the relationship between two variables and would be stated as a question to guide the research. In chapter 9, we will describe the different sampling techniques that need to be used depending upon whether you are conducting more quantitative research or hypothesis testing or whether your research question is more exploratory or qualitative.

The move from question to hypothesis development begins with a review of the published research. Existing research studies will quickly reveal that other researchers have described relationships between the variables in your study. Thus, they will define whether that relationship falls within two types of hypotheses that may be used to frame your study: directional hypothesis and non-directional hypothesis (see figure).

Types of Hypotheses

Directional

Directional hypotheses are those that indicate the direction in which the independent variable affects or is related to the dependent variable. Take, for instance, the hypothesis, "Involvement in community service is positively related to heightened reports of social responsibility among high school seniors." Here, the independent variable is community service and the dependent variable is social responsibility. The target population is high school seniors. In this example, the hypothesis states that being involved in community service will promote one's sense of social responsibility, or the propensity to use your abilities to improve your community.

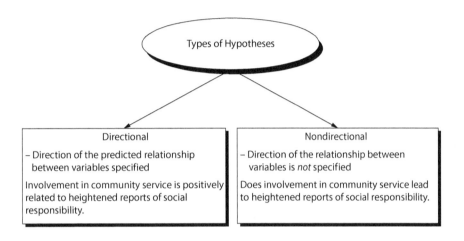

FIGURE 7.1 TYPES OF HYPOTHESES

Non-Directional

Non-directional hypotheses also include an independent and dependent variable, but the manner in which they are related is not specified. As such, non-directional hypotheses are stated in terms of a question. Thus, the hypothesis, "Does involvement in community service lead to heightened reports of social responsibility?" is unclear in terms of whether community service promotes social responsibility. Inconsistencies in previous research, investigations into newly developed programs or counseling strategies, or any other instance in which expected outcomes are unclear are times when a non-directional hypothesis may be stated. One should also note the structure of these two questions/statements. The first, directional hypothesis, is more of a statement that you are suspecting that by having community service projects, the participants will have a greater sense of social responsibility. The second, non-directional hypothesis, is exploring to see if there is that relationship. The difference may be that there has not been sufficient research on these two variables to provide a more definitive response as in the directional hypothesis. Thus, it is important to know the existing research to help in the determination of whether one variable has an effect on the other or whether you are exploring the effect that one has on the other.

Thus, one can state that using a directional or non-directional hypothesis will depend on many factors, including:

— results of prior studies
— theoretical perspective(s)
— professional wisdom

The use of hypothesis testing in the scientific process is a little peculiar, though. One does not accept or reject a hypothesis; rather, the decision is to accept or reject the null hypothesis. The null hypothesis is the inverse of the hypothesis. There can be many explanations for this, but I personally think that this relates to the fact that there are no exact sciences or theories that predict everything, as described in chapter 1. Therefore, rather than focusing the accuracy of your study on trying to prove your hypothesis, one creates a null hypothesis to accept or reject, thus maintaining the integrity of your hypothesis and only suggesting whether it should be accepted or rejected. This relates to the idea that inferential statistics (chapter 11) do not prove anything, but rather suggest or infer that a relationship is or is not what it appears as stated in the hypothesis. Thus, research that focuses on hypothesis testing does not prove anything, but only suggests relationships. The role of the null hypothesis suggesting relationships between variables in a study falls within the scope of quantitative research. Regardless of whether a directional or a non-directional hypothesis has been specified, the null hypothesis is always the same: there is no relationship between the independent and dependent variables, or that the independent variable does not impact/affect the dependent variable(s).

In regards to the hypothesis on the impact of community service on social responsibility, the null hypothesis would be that community service has no effect on social responsibility—regardless of whether the hypothesis is directional or non-directional. Thus, regardless of the hypothesis under consideration, the null hypothesis specifies that the independent and dependent variables are not related. As such, the null hypothesis serves as a basis to judge whether we accept the alternative hypothesis.

The alternative hypothesis is generally the statement that we seek to confirm. In consideration of our previous hypothesis on community service, the alternative hypothesis is the hypothesis, if stated in a directional sense—community service will promote one's sense of social responsibility. Therefore, regardless of if one states a directional or non-directional hypothesis, the alternative hypothesis specifies that the independent and dependent variables are related.

As becomes evident as one engages more in a body of literature, rarely do quantitative studies explicitly state the null hypothesis. Instead, the study hypothesis (if directional) is the alternative hypothesis—or the hypothesis the researcher seeks to confirm through data collection and analysis. Thus, the null hypothesis is implied but it is the alternative hypothesis that is reported.

Usable hypotheses, then, are those that:

1. State expected relationship between variables
2. are testable
3. are consistent with existing literature
4. are simple and concise

A word of caution: hypotheses are best-guess statements and should not be used for decision-making. Thus, there is a split between hypothesis-testing research and research that can be used for decision-making. If you are trying to determine the efficacy of a particular method, then you will not be using hypothesis testing, but rather looking at issues associated with cost-benefit analyses of implementation of the method. A program evaluation or use of some type of action research would be best considered to arrive at a type of research for decision-making. This will be discussed in more detail in the next chapter.

Hypothesis or Purpose for the Research

State your question _____

From your question and the literature search, identify the relationship between the variables in your question:

Identify how the literature has defined causal relationships between terms with the independent variable having an effect on the dependent variable. List the variables as defined by the literature.

Independent Variable   Dependent Variable

_____   _____

_____   _____

_____   _____

Restate your question in hypothesis form (specify whether it is directional or non-directional)

_____

For example, in the homeless shelter study, the literature about informal supports in senior centers described a positive correlation between informal supports and participant well-being (the more informal supports, the healthier the individual). Second, the literature on people who were homeless described a situation where the person who was homeless was devoid of supports, both formal and informal. Therefore, it was assumed that if supports can be provided to people who were homeless, then they can be used to address the problems of people who were homeless as they had with the elderly. This, then, was a conceptual non-directional hypothesis that would be trying to address whether there was a relationship between social supports and well-being for people who are homeless.

The difficult part was how to operationalize the conceptual hypothesis. On the one hand, it was easy to quantify the number of supports, both formal and informal, through a counting system. However, that did not identify the quality of that support. In addition, there was a problem with understanding the role of the shelter in creating supports that will last. Sure, the shelter can make a referral, but is there any guarantee that the referral would be kept? As you can begin to see, the research question about the role of shelters in addressing the problems of people who were home-less led to further questions. The beginning phase was quantifiable and did have a hypothesis. However, the findings from the initial phase of the study led to other questions where there was no hypothesis. These other questions, with no specific variables or measures, were the bulk of an exploratory study. The goal was to generate initial insights into the nature of the relationship between the shelter and the guests. None of the previous information was helpful in answering these questions, only confirmed the need to conduct a mixed methods research study. Therefore, many times quantitative research creates questions that need to be answered through a qualitative study, as described by the homeless shelter study. These are all design questions that will be addressed in the next chapter.

Before moving forward, to the best of your ability, look at the relationships between variables in your study and develop a hypothesis. Use the following form as a guide in the development of your hypothesis.

HYPOTHESES

Hypotheses require you to predict an answer to your question based on knowledge of the field, logical analysis based on theory, and/or anecdotal observations. Purely exploratory or descriptive studies do not require directional hypotheses but would rather explore the relationship between the variables and would generate a non-directional hypothesis. Even so, it is wise to commit yourself to a set of expectations regarding results.

State your question _____

_____

Describe how the variables in your question relate to each other.

_____is related to_____

_____ is related to_____

_____ is related to_____

_____ is related to_____

Therefore: (independent variable is related to the dependent variable)

_____

_____

Initial statement of hypotheses.

Conceptual Hypothesis: _____

_____

Operational Hypothesis: _____

_____

Are there any alternative relationships or explanations that serve as competing or rival hypotheses?

_____

_____

Revise your hypotheses considering (if possible) specific competing alternatives to the hypothesized relationships.

_____

_____

Research Design

To this point, there has been a lot of discussion about the reason for the study, the variables, the relationship between variables, and the hypothesis. Now you are ready to make the determination as to the type of study that you will be conducting. As mentioned above, there are some studies with non-directional hypotheses where you have two variables but it is unclear how one relates to the other. These studies are better suited for exploratory designs. In these instances, you are utilizing your observations, experiences, and interactions to define a process of intervention that can be tested at a later time. These designs are very individualized with small sample sizes that provide some insight to what is happening (more on sampling in the next chapter).

Experimental, Qualitative, Mixed Method Research

There are other studies that are explanatory, or they explain a relationship between variables. In an explanatory study, you are testing a directional hypothesis, as defined earlier. There are a number of ways that you can test your hypothesis. There is a true experimental design. The danger is that experimental designs are very difficult in the social sciences because you are dealing with human subjects. The closest human subjects study to an experimental design in recent history was the biosphere (a project that sequestered people in a biosphere for a number of years to see how they would survive). However, there are different ways of collecting data that may be quasi-experimental (still uses experimental design but does not have all the controls as a true experiment). For the sake of simplicity, the term experimental design will be used, but it will actually be referring to a quasi-experimental design. Other types of designs commonly used in human services are: survey; single subject; or a combination of the above. Human service workers are quite adept at designing research projects that will answer the question.

There is also the question of whether you will use qualitative methods or quantitative methods in conducting your research. The difference is in the type of information that you will be measuring. Quantitative measures are a way of counting information. Closed-ended surveys provide a good way of collecting quantitative data. Qualitative research involves the use of participant observation to understand the relationship that is taking place between variables. For the homeless shelter study, I used qualitative measures, which included field notes and interviews, to determine the relationship between the shelter, the guests, and the staff. I was not sure about the relationship between these three prior to the study, so there was a non-directional hypothesis for the study. The study was used to identify relationships that could be tested at a later time using quantitative measures. A general rule of thumb is that if your idea of what you want measured is clear and defined, then use quantitative measures. However, if you are uncertain as to the nature of the relationship, then qualitative measures are needed.

There are also mixed methods studies. These are studies when the researcher will use a combination of both quantitative data (statistical trends) and qualitative data (stories, interviews, etc.) (Creswell, 2015). Mixed methods research does carry a level of rigor with it. Mixed methods research will fall under one of three categories. *Convergent design* is where both quantitative and qualitative data is analyzed and merged with the purpose of comparing results. *Explanatory sequential design* is where the intent is to first use quantitative methods to identify relationships and then use qualitative methods to explain the relationships in greater detail. *Exploratory sequential design* is the third type. This is where the researcher first explores the relationship between the variables using qualitative methods to gain an understanding of the relationship between them and then builds on the qualitative finding through quantitative measures (Creswell, 2015, pg. 6).

As stated in the first chapter, one form of research builds on the other. Therefore, both quantitative and qualitative research measures are important in social work. One thing to think about is that since the relationship between variables is clear in a quantitative study, the information is easier to analyze at the analysis stage of the study (the back end). A lot of thought goes into the study before you reach that point, but the data is definitely easier to analyze.

Qualitative research is the opposite. Since the relationship between variables is vague, you have generalized questions that you want to test. This means that there are many open-ended questions where you try to identify trends. The front end of this type of research is easier, but it is the back end, or the analysis phase, where one puts in the work. This is where the researcher is sifting through mountains of data to identify trends between sources of data. Focus groups, interviews, case notes, participant observation, etc. are some of the sources of qualitative data that may be used. More on analyzing data in a later section; this section is to help you establish a design to be used to collect the data.

To provide some of the basic components of an experimental design while being sensitive to human subjects, social scientists use a quasi-experimental design. This type provides the basic concepts of experimentation (with experimental and control groups) but the researcher does not have the total control over the environment to guarantee similarities between experimental and control subjects as in a true experimental design.

Technically, an experiment can be defined as a "scientific investigation in which the researcher manipulates one or more independent variables, controls any other relevant variables and observes the effect of the manipulations on the dependent variable(s)" (Ary, Jacobs, and Razavieh, 2002, p. 276). As provided, particular focus is on how changes to the independent variable may subsequently affect the dependent variable(s). Take, for example, the following question: Do professor-developed formative assessments lead to increased student achievement? The formative assessments are the independent variable and academic achievement is the dependent variable (DV). We could measure the independent variable (IV) by assigning professors to either work together to develop their own classroom-based formative assessments or do not use such assessments (referred to as the control group). Or a third condition could be included in the study in which professors are required to use publisher-developed formative assessments. The DV could be measured through some achievement measure, such as an achievement or end-of-course exam score.

Within this example, the IV was actively manipulated by the researcher—use of formative assessment data. Oftentimes, however, we are not offered the luxury of manipulating the IV, such as when students are already grouped according to a class or according to demographics, such as sex, race/ethnicity, and/or neighborhood.

In such cases, the research question(s) of interest may be focused on whether group differences exist on some outcome, such as reading comprehension or perception toward professional knowledge. To be more specific, the research question may be whether there are racial/ethnic group differences on perceived sense of professional ethics within the profession between different student groups. In this case, the researcher cannot manipulate one's race/ethnicity, it is predetermined. Here, then, the IV is race/ethnicity and the DV is the outcome variable, or sense of professional ethics. Therefore, this research question is investigated by comparing pre-existing groups (gender, socioeconomic) on some outcome variable.

Experimental research designs

We will consider a range of experimental designs. As will be evident, there are a host of experimental designs that can be selected to address a given research question. Which design to use depends on various factors, including: research question(s), target population (or its size, large or small), and accessible population, among other factors. Regardless, characteristics of experiments are:

- observation—using defensible approaches to investigate whether changes in the DV can be attributed to the IV
- manipulation of the environment—investigating the degree to which changes in the environment result in changes in another variable
- efforts to control extraneous influences that might limit or bias observations—that is, identify variables that may impact the DV above and beyond that attributed to the IV. For example, prior academic achievement or motivation may be extraneous variables that impact student outcomes and comprehension above and beyond other program involvement.

Other key concepts you should already be aware of include: independent variable, dependent variable, control variable (one that ensures that the only differences between your experimental and comparison groups are differences on the IV, not some pre-existing differences), and extraneous variable (one that may affect your dependent variable above and beyond the IV). In the above example, prior achievement and motivation are extraneous variables that may impact academic achievement above and beyond educational participation. Extraneous variables are also called covariates and should always be considered when conducting and reading social science research. The intent of an experimental design is to measure the change that the IV has on the DV independent of other factors. This is called manipulation of the DV.

This may be described as a simple two-group design where you have an experimental group and a control group. Thus, it is the experimental group that receives the intervention and the control group does not. To guarantee for similarity between the two groups, there would be random assignment to each of the groups. First, measurements would be taken of both groups before any intervention to determine the similarities between the groups. Then the intervention would be completed. Following the intervention, the difference between groups would be measured. The assumption being that the only difference between the two groups would be the intervention that was conducted. Thus, the difference between the two groups would show the effect of the intervention. This is depicted by the diagram below.

Random Assignment	Group	Treatment	Posttest
(R)	E	X	Y2
(R)	C	--	Y2

FIGURE 8.1 RANDOMIZED SUBJECT, POSTTEST-ONLY CONTROL GROUP DESIGN

Random Assignment

Random assignment is mentioned as the ideal to overcome threats of internal validity (discussed later in this chapter) of experimenter bias—that is, after participants are randomly assigned to groups, any differences that exist between groups is due to chance factors alone, not systematic experimenter bias (e.g., intentionally putting all higher-achieving students in after-school program).

Unfortunately, in some cases, we cannot randomly assign individuals to comparison groups. That is, to look at the effect of a particular instructional strategy, it is not feasible to pull participants from their lives to randomly assign them to different groups.

Instead, it is more feasible to impose a particular treatment on a group of participants, such as a particular location or clinics. Experimental designs that seek to manipulate the IV by imposing conditions on intact groups are quasi-experimental designs.

One example of a quasi-experimental design is if one was interested in looking at the effect of a character program for reducing school violence. In this case, two comparable schools in terms of SES and student demographics could be used. Here, the character program, such as Positive Behavior Interventions and Supports (PBIS), would be imposed on one or more schools with other schools not receiving the program (control groups) to investigate reduction in school violence. Again, ensuring comparable groups is critical, as one does not want pre-existing factors influencing how the DV is impacted by the IV.

There may be times when you are not able to utilize an experimental design model to answer your research question. It does not mean that you throw away the rigor of the research; rather, there are additional precautions to address potential threats to validity. One such model is a single-subject design, which is what I would say is something that is used in a clinical process in determining whether the intervention you are using is effective or not.

A single-subject design model is in essence a one-group pre-test post-test design. In this case, one person or one group of individuals is selected into a study to see if a particular intervention (such as cognitive behavioral therapy) may effectively promote positive individual outcome changes (reduced anxiety). As shown, the group is selected and administered a pre-test, subsequently exposed to the treatment (therapy) and then assessed on the post-test. The premise is that any pre- and post-test score changes are due to exposure to the IV (therapy).

Pretest	Intervention	Posttest
Y1	X	Y2

FIGURE 8.2 ONE-GROUP PRETEST-POSTTEST DESIGN

Pre-Test/Posttest

Another single-subject design model would be a static group comparison design. As shown below, this design builds on the just discussed single-group design by including a control group and excluding a pre-test. Thus, the ability to ascertain change is determined by factors that happen in relationship to a comparison group/individual or even something that might be identified by normal change factors in the literature. Issues of threats to internal validity will be discussed later in this section.

Group	IV	Posttest
E	X	Y2
C	--	Y2

FIGURE 8.3 STATIC GROUP COMPARISON

A reason for considering an experimental design for your study is to address potential threats to internal validity. Remember, the goal of the study is to measure as closely as possible the outcome resulting from the intervention being tested; therefore, it is important to control for factors that could affect that outcome measure. Some threats to validity include: pretesting, maturation, history, experimenter bias, and so on (these will be introduced below). Pre-testing effects come into play here because participants may be made aware of study intent due to the questions, perhaps influencing post-test examination.

Maturation effects could come into play here because participants dealing with anxiety, perhaps due to the loss of a loved one, may naturally adapt to their loss. History is a factor because participants may be dealing with anxiety through other avenues besides therapeutic exposure.

Therefore, when threats to validity potentially play into the information gathered from a study, then it is not an acceptable experimental design. True experimental designs are unique in that participants are randomly assigned to treatment conditions, such as exposing social science college students to receive one-on-one research tutoring or not to see whether this results in changes in research comprehension. Again, the idea is that after random assignment, any existing group differences are attributed to chance factors and not experimenter bias. As such, they are considered the "gold standard" in experimental design.

Here is a graphical representation of such as design, or the randomized subject, post-test only control group design. As shown, groups are based on random assignment (R) and no pre-test is administered. Both random assignment and no pre-test are designed to minimize threats to internal validity. This particular design is the most desirable design for inferential statistical hypothesis testing, as groups can be considered equal (due to random assignment) and participants are not exposed to pre-testing. Thus, any observed post-test score differences can be attributed to treatment exposure.

Random Assignment	Group	Treatment	Posttest
(R)	E	X	Y2
(R)	C	--	Y2

FIGURE 8.4 RANDOMIZED SUBJECT, POST-TEST ONLY CONTROL GROUP DESIGN

Another experimental design is called the randomized subject, pre-test post-test group design. Like the previous design, participants are randomly assigned to groups. However, unlike before, treatment groups are administered a pre-test in addition to the post-test. Pre-testing may be desirable when the research question deals with looking at factors associated with increases in participant change over time, or in helping to establish a baseline. However, pre-testing can be a threat to internal validity that one must consider. Nonetheless, this is a defensible experimental design for hypothesis testing in social science research.

For instances in which random assignment is still feasible and one wants to ensure comparable groups on relevant variables, such as gender, race/ethnicity, and/or achievement, the "randomized matched subjects, post-test only control group design" can be used.

Random	Group	Pretest	Treatment	Posttest
(R)	E	Y1	X	Y2
(R)	C	Y1	--	Y2

FIGURE 8.5 RANDOMIZED SUBJECT, PRE-TEST POST-TEST GROUP DESIGN

Randomized Subject, Pre-test Post-test Group Design

Here, participants are matched up as closely as possible on relevant variables. Then, once matched, the participants are randomly assigned to one of the treatment conditions. That is, if you have two individuals match by gender and achievement, one member would be randomly assigned to one group and the other assigned to the comparison group. Like the previously discussed design, this design overcomes pre-test threats, as only a post-test is used as a measure of the DV (changes in academic achievement, depression, etc.).

Solomon three-group design

Less used experimental designs are the Solomon designs. First is the "Solomon three-group design," which includes a treatment group that receives a pre- and post-test in addition to exposure to the intervention (e.g., one-on-one tutoring). As shown, the first control group only is administered the pre- and post-test, but no intervention. The second control is exposed to the treatment and is then administered the post-test. The idea of this design is to determine the degree to which pre-testing may impact post-test scores.

Random	Group	Pretest	Treatment	Posttest
(R)	E	Y1	X	Y2
(R)	C1	Y1	--	Y2
(R)	C2	--	X	Y2

FIGURE 8.6 SOLOMON THREE-GROUP DESIGN

Solomon four-group design

The "Solomon four-group design" is an extension of this and includes a treatment group and three distinct control groups. As shown, the experimental group is administered the pre- and post-test and is exposed to the treatment (e.g., cognitive behavioral therapy). Contrary, the first control group is only administered the pre- and post-test; the second control group receives exposure to the treatment and is administered the post-test; last, the third control group is only administered the post-test.

Random	Group	Pretest	Treatment	Posttest
(R)	E	Y1	X	Y2
(R)	C1	Y1	--	Y2
(R)	C2	--	X	Y2
(R)	C3	--	--	Y2

FIGURE 8.7 SOLOMON FOUR-GROUP DESIGN

The aim of these designs is to investigate the degree to which specific threats to internal validity may affect the DV above and beyond the IV (treatment). Despite their strengths to addressing social science research questions, they may not be feasible in many social science research settings due to the difficulty in having enough study participants to assign to each experimental condition.

Reliability and Validity

As we have discussed in relationship to research designs, there are many factors to consider when preparing to engage in social science research. In particular, researchers and consumers of research alike must consider factors that may affect the DV above and beyond the IV. Because social science research is commonly situated in clinical settings, we must be mindful of the factors that affect the outcomes we seek to promote. This is aligned with identifying threats to both internal and external validity.

To begin, there are two research terms that are somewhat confusing, reliability and validity. I like to think of the two as something like shooting at a target. The target to the left is scattered all over and as such is not reliable or valid. The middle target has all the points clustered but not in the bullseye. As such, it would be considered reliable but not valid. However, the target on the right is showing that there is consistency in the bullseye area. This suggests that it is both valid and reliable. Simply put, validity answers the questions that you want answered, and reliability is the consistency of those responses.

Thus, when discussing internal validity, we are dealing with whether changes in the DV can be attributed because of the interaction of the IV. The consistency of that change means that the interaction with the IV would be reliable. Whether or not study findings can be generalized to other population sub-groups and contexts outside of the study parameters addresses issues with external validity. The three concepts are serious issues that should be considered when conducting and evaluating published research.

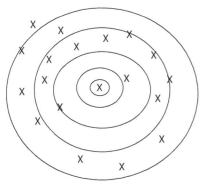

Is this reliable? Is this valid?

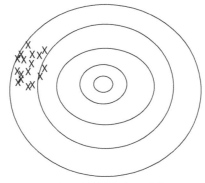

Is this reliable? Is this valid?

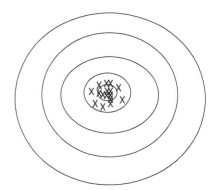

Is this reliable? Is this valid?

FIGURE 8.8A, FIGURE 8.8B, & FIGURE 8.8C RELIABILITY & VALIDITY

As alluded to above, the design of your study is an important way to address threats to validity. As mentioned, validity is a term referring to whether the scores are measuring what they were designed to measure. Internal validity, then, specifically addresses whether the degree to which observed changes in the dependent variable can be attributed to changes caused by the independent variable.

Take, for example, the hypothesis that a one-on-one research tutoring program will promote improved student learning outcomes in research. However, if those involved in the tutoring program are highly motivated to achieve academically (more so than those not in the program), this may pose a threat to internal validity—that is, motivation is a confounding variable that may impact academic achievement above and beyond the effects of participating in the tutoring program. This deals with the threat of selection-maturation, where the selected sample may be unique in some way (e.g., achievement motivation).

Threats to internal validity

There are many types of threats to internal validity. Here is a partial list of identifiable threats to internal validity:

History is a threat to internal validity and involves events or conditions that happen *at the same time* as the experiment. History is a threat to internal validity because individual behavior is influenced by involvement in a range of activities and/or programs. For example, although the tutoring program participation may promote academic achievement, some students may also be receiving additional remediation instruction from a classmate or friend. Here, although the treatment group includes the tutoring program, involvement in other activities to promote learning may also help explain increases in student achievement above and beyond the IV.

Maturation relates to naturally occurring changes (biological or psychological) in the subjects that happen during the course of the study. Maturation is another threat to internal validity because individuals naturally develop (psychologically, physically) without involvement in a particular intervention. For example, the effects of a physical education program on first-grade students' physical outcomes may be reduced because students become more coordinated and stronger with age. Thus, it is reasonable to ask whether students' improved coordination and strength was due to the physical education program or to naturally occurring changes.

Pre-test may influence post-test performance. Pre-test is another threat because it deals with the fact that if one was looking at achievement growth gains prior to and after intervention involvement, pre-test exposure may influence post-test performance. This ties into practice effects—the more times you take a test, the better you may perform.

Instrumentation scales need to show evidence of reliability and validity. Post-tests should not be easier than pre-tests. Instrumentation is another threat to internal validity. Here, as previously discussed, obtained scores must show acceptable levels of reliability and validity to serve useful. In the event that test scores report low reliability, those scores cannot be used to derive conclusions on intervention efficacy. This is the case because score variance reflects error more than reliable variance or that due to actual ability level.

Statistical regression such as high or low scores will generally regress toward the overall group mean on subsequent tests. This means that statistical regression deals with the observation that if a group scores considerably high on a measure, they have nowhere else to go but down, whereas those scoring low have nowhere to go but up. Consider, for example, that you take a test and do better than expected. In most cases, you're better not to take the exam again, because it is likely your score will regress down toward the overall group mean. Another way to think about it is when I was on a bowling league. In the first week, we established our base average for the league that would be used for establishing our handicap. What that meant was that if my handicap score was high and I did not achieve that score, then we would actually lose points to the other team. However, if my average started off low and I showed progress throughout the season, then it was better for our team since we started with a lower handicap score.

Some additional threats to internal validity are:

- Differential selection of subjects
    - important differences between subjects in experimental and control groups
    - For instance, one group composed of seniors and the other of juniors
- Experimental mortality
    - differential loss, or attrition, of participants from the comparison groups
- Selection-maturation interaction
    - selection process and maturation of students over course of study may limit the accuracy of results
- Experimenter effect
    - unintentional effects (e.g., personal bias) brought into study by investigator
- Subject effects
    - the attitudes and perspectives brought into study by subjects
    - Some types may include:
- Hawthorne effect
    - tendency of subjects to alter their behavior because they know they are being observed
- John Henry effect, or compensatory rivalry

- tendency of control group to exert extra effort and, thus, increase their performance
- Diffusion
    - subjects in one group communicate information of study to subjects in another group

While it is not necessary to consider every threat to internal validity when reading and engaging in research, one should identify those that may be of most relevance to the study at hand. In such cases, it is critical to consider how the study author(s) may or may not have addressed a particular threat. Failure to acknowledge potential threats to internal validity may result in a study with little to no practical implications.

Overcoming Threats to Internal Validity

Although not all the previously mentioned threats to internal validity will necessarily affect each and every study, they are factors to consider. That is, the list should not be considered a checklist to overcome. Instead, those engaging in and reading social science research should consider how these threats to internal validity may affect study findings and implications. Indeed, some threats may be more relevant to one study than another, and thus, the researcher(s) should design the study to address any potential threats.

This flowchart provides strategies for overcoming potential threats to internal validity. One way to overcome potential threats to internal validity includes randomly selecting study participants from the population. The idea here is that randomly selecting individuals to participate in a study will reduce subject effects (or pre-existing differences that individuals may bring into the study). However, as previously discussed, we are often not able to randomly select individuals from clinical settings, since we typically use convenient sampling methods by selecting intact groups of subject or clinics.

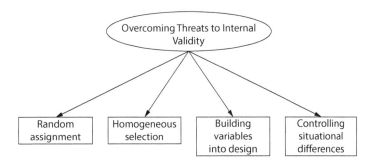

FIGURE 8.9 OVERCOMING THREATS TO INTERNAL VALIDITY

Alternatively, homogeneous selection could be used by recruiting participants with shared characteristics. Such characteristics could include: levels of depression, academic achievement, parent education level, programs serving similar socioeconomic status, etc.

Another strategy is building variables into the experimental design. As discussed above, it is possible to account for extraneous variables, or covariates, into the experimental design to account for pre-existing differences between compared groups (treatment vs. control). To revisit a prior example on the effects of after-school program participation on academic achievement among third-grade students, a possible covariate could be prior academic achievement in second grade. Here, those in the after-school program may have had higher second-grade GPAs than those in the control group (no program involvement). Based on this pre-existing difference between groups, it is possible to still make meaningful comparisons between the groups on the DV (academic achievement) by accounting for prior achievement differences.

Lastly, another strategy is controlling situational differences between treatment and control groups. This could be done by focusing on one location instead of multiple locations, or conducting a study in one neighborhood or those with similar resources (proximity to park, gas stations, liquor stores, etc.). This will control contextual factors (e.g., SES) on the DV.

Threats to External Validity

Whereas threats to internal validity deal with attributing changes in the DV by the IV, another type of threat is that to external validity. Threats to external validity deal with the degree to which study findings can be generalized to other contexts and population sub-groups. Therefore, there are two types of threats to internal validity. The first is:

- Population External Validity
  - Or, the interaction between subject characteristics and treatment, which deals specifically with how subjects are selected into the study. Specifically, subjects should be representative of the population that results are intended to be generalized to; if not, this limitation must be addressed in the study.

The second type is:

- Ecological Validity
  - The issue here is the generalization of results to other situations/contexts. For example, one must consider the instance in which promising results on a particular intervention were found based on a sample of individuals from the Midwest and the likelihood of similar results being obtained in the California Central Valley. Factors that may hinder ecological validity include:
  - pre-test may sensitize subjects to treatment
  - subjects' attitudes and feelings may influence the effect that the independent variable may have on them
  - a novel effect may produce a positive result only because it is novel
  - experimenter effect

Overcoming Threats to External Validity

Similar to overcoming threats to internal validity, there are specific ways in which those associated with external validity can be addressed. Five strategies are provided here:

1. One approach is the random selection of study participants from the target or accessible population. The process of random selection minimizes potential experimenter bias in selecting individuals to be in a study, as well as promotes the likelihood that study participants will represent the larger population. Within this strategy, having a large sample size will promote the likelihood that the sample represents the population, such as in terms of important characteristics: sex, race/ethnicity, SES, etc.

2. A second strategy that can be used includes integrating participant characteristics into the study. This can occur, for example, if one was looking at the effects of one-on-one tutoring for research students' research fluency. A potential participant trait could be the risk of the student—either a high-risk student or low-risk student. Using this information, the researcher could include tutoring methodologies as an independent variable to see whether the one-on-one tutoring is more effective for promoting research fluency among high-risk students than those identified as low-risk. One can easily see how this could generalize to other personal characteristics, such as sex or race/ethnicity. That is, oftentimes it may be of interest to see if an intervention will be more beneficial to certain individuals than others.

3. Another potential strategy is using experimental designs that take into account threats to internal validity to address the risks to external validity. One approach is a design in which a pre-test is not needed, thus reducing practice effect. Also, the use of two control groups could be used— for example, one receives a pre-test and another does not. This would enable one to determine the degree to which exposure to a pre-test may impact post-test scores.

4. The fourth approach mentioned here deals with using clear operational definitions of study variables. In this instance, instead of developing one's own measures for spelling or word recognition, a norm-referenced standardized test could be adopted to measure learning

outcomes associated with language arts. This would minimize factors associated with instrumentation since published tests have undergone thorough development and review processes to promote reliable and valid scores. It also ties into the final factor addressed here, replication.

5. Replication is an important way to address threats to external validity. The aim of replication is conducting the same study in a different context or with a different target population to see if findings are similar to the study in which it was based. For example, a study that found providing students with immediate feedback on task performance improved the academic achievement of college students should be replicated across various colleges to test the robustness of study findings. It is certainly not advisable to adopt a new program without first testing whether purported outcomes are expected based on the research in which the program is based.

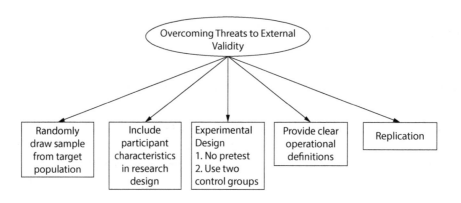

FIGURE 8.10 OVERCOMING THREATS TO EXTERNAL VALIDITY

Although not exhaustive, these five strategies are ways in which one can address threats to external validity.

ELIMINATING PROCEDURAL BIAS

Bias refers to sources of systematic error that may affect study results. Unless adequately controlled, bias may render your results non-interpretable. With a general protocol in mind, specific attention should be given to each of the following potential sources of bias. The design should evolve as you add controls for the most serious of these. Those mentioned below are adapted from *Experimental and Quasi-Experimental Design for Research*, Campbell, D.T. and Stanley, J.C., Ravenio Books 2015.

State your hypothesis _____

_____.

1. **Effects of Historical Events**—Anticipate events such as personnel changes, environmental events, interference by nonparticipants, etc., that will take place during your data collection phase that might affect the results. (Describe problem and how you will address it)

   _____

   _____

   _____

2. **Effects of Maturation**—If subjects are to be observed over time, are there changes that might result merely by normal development, growth, natural course of illness, etc.? (Describe problem and how you will address it)

   _____

   _____

   _____

3. **Effects of Repeated Measurement**—If the same measurements are repeated on subjects, will subjects likely remember past responses, prepare differently for the next session, or relax procedures?
   (Describe problem and how you will address it)

   _____

   _____

4. **Instrument Decay**—Is it likely that test equipment will wear out, observers get bored, protocols get short-cut by investigators, etc.?
(Describe problem and how you will address it)

_____

_____

5. **Effects of Statistical Regression**—If subjects are chosen because they lie at the extremes of a distribution (e.g., extreme anxiety, low compliance with therapy), subsequent measurements will tend to be more nearly average for purely statistical reasons. Describe how you will select to avoid this problem.

_____

_____

6. **Subject Selection**—Is there anything in the selection of your sample or assignment of subjects to groups that makes one group of subjects unintentionally different from other groups? For example, does your study represent bias toward race, gender, class, sexual preference, or social desirability?   (Describe how you will avoid the problem)

_____

_____

7. **Loss of Subjects**—Subjects lost to attrition may be different from those who remain. How does your study control for this possibility? (Describe how you will avoid the problem)

_____

_____

_____

8. **Investigator Bias**—How will you avoid influencing subjects by your attention, attitude, etc.? (Describe how you will avoid the problem)

_____

_____

_____

Reliability

Reliability deals with test score consistency. Specifically, if one could hypothetically take a test an infinite number of times, the obtained score would fall within a specific range (low, middle, or high range). That is, one's scores after repeatedly taking the test should vary only due to random error. In theory, it would not make sense for the same individual to obtain very different scores if tested repeatedly on the same test.

Validity, on the other hand, deals with whether obtained scores on a survey/test represent the trait (motivation, depression, academic achievement) it was designed to measure. Importantly, when talking about reliability and validity, we are dealing with obtained scores, not the test itself, thus addressing problems with validity as systemic issues as identified above, whereas problems with reliability are a result of error.

Thus, even though a study may report acceptable levels of reliability based on test scores obtained from a sample of college students, scores from the same test when obtained from a group of high school students may not be as reliable for a number of reasons, such as inappropriate reading level of items. Therefore, reliability and validity must be considered whenever scores are obtained from a given sample.

Therefore, it is not the test that is reliable/valid, but the actual test scores. This is because the scores serve as the source of information for decision-making purposes, such as evaluating program efficacy or program planning.

Reliability deals with test score consistency. As previously stated, if you were to take a test a number of times, the extent to which your score fluctuates from time to time deals with reliability. If scores were reliable, your scores across repeated times would essentially be the same, with the exception of random error. On the other hand, low reliability would occur if your score was to fluctuate to the extent that you obtained a high score on the first test and a low score on the next, and so on. Here, the low reliability would have serious implications on how your score could be interpreted. Essentially, low reliability indicates a high degree of error, whereas high reliability indicates that the variability of scores is due to reliable (actual trait) variance, not error.

Quantitatively, reliability values range from 0 to 1.00, with higher values indicating more acceptable levels of reliability. Essentially, reliability values indicate the amount of variance in scores due to reliable variance (or free of error). Or, to put it in another way, it indicates the degree of variance in scores due to reliable variance. For example, a reliability value of .85 would indicate that 85 percent of the variance in scores is reliable and 15 percent of the variance is attributable to error. Likewise, a reliability of .90 would indicate that 10 percent of score variance is due to some type of error (perhaps unclear questions). Across educational, clinical, and vocational testing contexts, it is desirable to have reliabilities that exceed .80.

Based on the purposes of testing, reliability can be assessed in a number of ways. Three types of reliability considered here include: internal consistency, test-retest (deals with test score stability), and alternate forms (deals with test score equivalency). Although each assesses reliability in a different way, they all share the same aim to determine the degree to which scores are free of error.

Reliability, as we have discussed, deals with the degree to which a test yields consistent scores. Internal reliability is one type of reliability that deals with the extent to which items on a scale produce consistent scores. It addresses the question of, "Do the items function together to produce a consistent score to operationalize a measured trait, such as motivation or academic achievement?" Thus, internal reliability can be determined based on a single administration of an instrument.

Empirical research supports the use of scores with internal reliability estimates equal to or above .80. The two most commonly reported internal reliability measures are: Cronbach's coefficient alpha (or just alpha) and Kuder-Richardson 20. Cronbach's alpha is appropriate for dichotomous (correct/incorrect) or ordered categorical items (Strongly Disagree—Strongly Agree). Whenever a published study employs some self-report measure, one should expect to see Cronbach's coefficient alpha reported, which should exceed .80. Typically, you will not see values less than .70 in published research, as this indicates that 30 percent of the variance in scores is due to error.

Kuder-Richardson, on the other hand, is used as an estimate of reliability for dichotomously scored items, such as those commonly found on an academic achievement test (correct/incorrect). Thus, it is most often reported for achievement or intelligence tests where items are scored as either correct or incorrect.

Regardless of which type of reliability is reported, internal reliability should be estimated and reported whenever scores are obtained on a group of individuals, because it is based on the characteristics of the instrument and sample. Thus, reliability in this context is group-dependent; in other words, reliability can change based on the characteristics of the sample. Another type of reliability is test-retest, used whenever a test is to be used at different time intervals (Time 1, Time 2). Test-retest reliability, therefore, deals with the degree to which an instrument yields consistent scores over time. Thus, if one was administered an IQ test today and obtained a score of 110 (ten points above mean) and then, following a three-week interval, obtained a score of 112, the correlation of these scores would indicate the test-retest reliability value.

Therefore, test-retest reliabilities are reported as a correlation coefficient, which ranges between -1 and $+1$. Correlations closer to $+1$ are desired, indicating that the scores obtained from the separate testing occasions are more similar.

Alternate forms of reliability deal with the equivalency of two test forms designed to be used interchangeably. For example, many large-scale published tests include two alternate forms, such as Form A and Form B, and include such tests as the Woodcock Johnson Tests of Achievement or any norm-referenced IQ test. The idea of developing alternate forms of the same test is that they can be administered within a short time interval if additional testing is needed. This could occur, for example, if one was administering an IQ test (Form A) and the ability to overcome external distractions (noise from street construction) proved to be an insurmountable task. In this case, testing could be discontinued and resumed the next day, if needed, using the alternate form (Form B).

Like test-retest reliability, alternate form reliability is estimated by correlating scores obtained from the alternate test forms. Thus, a high correlation (above .85) is desirable, indicating that scores can be interpreted similarly across test forms.

Factors Affecting Reliability

Because reliability provides a measure of the degree to which scores are error-free, there are many factors that introduce error into individual scores. The three domains in which errors could affect scores are provided in this flowchart and include error associated with the test itself, testing conditions, and examinees.

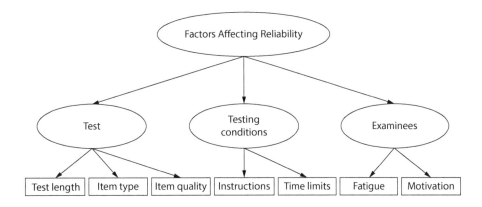

FIGURE 8.11 FACTORS AFFECTING RELIABILITY

One source of error is from the instrument itself, in the form of its length (short or long test), item type (subjectively or objectively scored), and item quality (clear, concise). Benefits are that longer tests provide the opportunity to use more items to assess a given trait; longer tests are more reliable than short tests. Item quality deals with the characteristics of the item. Items that are double-barreled reduce reliability because they are confusing and less clear to the respondent; thus, each item should be a clear statement that measures only one attribute of the individual.

Item type deals with whether the item is subjectively or objectively scored. Objectively scored items are more reliable than subjectively scored items, because there is no ambiguity in terms of an examinee's response. In this case, it is easy to determine how a respondent provided their answer on a rating scale or whether they got the item correct or incorrect. Subjectively scored items are also less reliable because they may be contaminated with rater effects. The halo effect is one factor that reduces reliability because the reported score includes the perceptions of the examinee on behalf of the rater in addition to ability level.

The conditions of administration introduce additional factors that may also affect reliability. For example, instructions on a test that are confusing may result in examinee frustration, thus introducing score error and reducing reliability. Whenever administering an instrument to a group of respondents, directions for completing it should be clear and concise. Additionally, time limits may affect reliability as well. For example, an overly restrictive time limit to complete a test may result in examinees providing answers on a whim without reviewing their accuracy. Here, the examinee is more concerned with just completing the test instead of applying knowledge of concepts.

Examinee factors also impact reliability. For example, a long test may result in examinee fatigue, lowering the possibility that the individual will put forth his/her best effort to do well, such as checking their answers. Also, examinees not motivated to perform well will invariably lead to lower reliability, because they are not putting forth the effort to do their best on the test. All these factors should be considered when selecting, designing, and administering any type of assessment—classroom assessment to clinical measure of depression or anxiety.

Standard Error of Measurement

When administering a test, it is desirable to have some index to characterize the amount of error present in examinees'/individuals' scores. Just as we use the standard error of the mean to determine the representativeness of the sample mean as an approximation of the population mean, we can use the standard error of measurement as an estimate of the degree to which one's observed score (X) represents the true score (T).

Conceptually, the standard error of measurement is the standard deviation of a group of individuals' scores across an infinite number of test administrations (motivation, academic achievement). That is, if a group of examinees (e.g., classroom of students) was to hypothetically take a test an infinite number of times, a distribution (or histogram) could be generated to graphically show the variation in scores across times. Remember, the average score of repeated tests would be the examinees' true score. The standard deviation of all examinees' scores across repeated tests would be the standard error of measurement. Thus, the standard error of measurement serves to provide an estimate of how well one's observed score reflects their true score, which is a hypothetical entity that we seek to estimate.

The standard error of measurement is approximated by subtracting the reliability of the scores (e.g., Cronbach's coefficient alpha) from 1.00, which indicates the amount of error, and then take its square root. Next, this value is multiplied by the standard deviation to yield an estimate of the standard error of measurement. Let's plug in some real numbers to more fully understand it.

Say a test was administered and had a reported standard deviation of 10 and a reliability of .85. Subtracting .85 from 1 and taking the square root provides an answer of .387. Multiplying it by 10 yields a standard error of measurement of 3.87. To see how higher reliability results in a lower standard error of measurement; we can recalculate the standard error of measurement based on a reliability of .93. In this case, the standard error of measurement is 2.65, which is lower than that based on a reliability of .85. This indicates that one's observed score will more likely represent the true score when test score reliability is high (closer to 1.00).

The utility of the standard error of measurement occurs when we want to make general statements about how confident we are in using the observed score to represent one's true score. Thus, we can use the standard error of measurement to generate confidence intervals around one's observed score. Confidence intervals are useful because they acknowledge that test scores are fallible and that one's score on an instrument can fluctuate from one testing occasion to another.

Confidence Intervals using SEMs

The use of confidence intervals using the standard error of measurement is designed to report the degree to which an individual's observed score represents the true score. Thus, confidence intervals require using the standard error of measurement to make statements about the likelihood that an individual's true score would fall within a particular score band around the examinee's observed score. There are three levels at which a confidence interval can be estimated and reported. These confidence levels include: 68 percent, 95 percent, and 99 percent (as reflected by one, two, or three standard deviations from the mean). These three levels deal with the extent to which one seeks to use an individual's observed score to reflect the true score. As such, these three levels are based on the assumption that one's distribution of scores obtained over repeated tests would be normally distributed (scores centered around some mean). Based on the premise that one's score distribution would be normally distributed over repeated tests, it would be expected that 68 percent of their scores would fall +/−1 standard deviation (or standard error of measurement) away from the mean, which is represented by the observed score. Similarly, 95 percent of an examinee's scores would fall between +/−2 standard error of the measurement, and 99 percent of scores would fall between +/−3 standard error of measurement from the observed score, respectively.

Let's consider a concrete example to show how the standard error of measurement is used in practice to generate confidence intervals around an examinee's score. Using the standard error of measurement of 2.65 previously obtained, the examinee's observed score (or X) is 98. It is of interest to estimate the likelihood that the true score falls around this score. To obtain a 68 percent confidence interval (one standard deviation), one simply multiplies the standard error of measurement by 1 to obtain 2.65, which is then added and subtracted from the observed score of 98 to obtain the interval 95.35 to 100.65. We can interpret this by saying, "There is a 68 percent likelihood that the examinee's true score falls between 95.35 and 100.65." This statement acknowledges the fallibility of test scores and that the score may fluctuate over repeated tests.

At the 95 percent confidence level, we multiply 2.65 (the SEM) by 1.96 to obtain 5.19, which is then added and subtracted from the observed score of 98. In this case, we can say that there is a 95 percent likelihood that the examinee's true score falls between 92.81 and 103.19. As such, the higher the confidence level, the wider the score band.

Lastly, at the 99 percent confidence level, the standard error of measurement of 2.65 is multiplied by 2.54 to obtain 6.73, which is then added and subtracted from the observed score of 98. In this example, then, we can say that there is a 99 percent likelihood that the examinee's true score falls between 91.27 and 104.73. Which confidence level to use depends on the test being administered, as well as one's desired level of certainty that the observed score captures the true score.

As implied in these examples, the lower the standard error of measurement, the more likely the observed score reflects the true score due to higher reliability. Confidence intervals are recommended to be reported to assist with communicating examinees' test performance. They can be estimated for any type of survey/test, and one only needs to have estimates of the standard deviation and reliability to estimate the standard error of measurement and, subsequently, confidence intervals.

Improving Reliability

Due to the effect of error on reliability and test score interpretation, it is extremely important to consider strategies to reduce the impact of error in social science measurement. First, items should be clear and measure only one attribute of the measured trait. Items should be reviewed by those familiar with the trait, being measured for clarity and to eliminate potentially offensive language. Second, instructions should be unambiguous and respondents should fully understand how to answer each question. Specifically, instructions should communicate the purpose(s) of the instrument, how much time is required to complete it, and be age/grade appropriate.

To ensure comparable scores, the conditions of testing should be as consistent across the examinees as much possible. Within group testing settings, this is more attainable when the test administrator can read the directions and all examinees take the instrument at the same time. This is demonstrated by classroom exams in which all students are administered a quiz/test that measures the same content domain, such as English language or mathematics, under the same conditions. Standardized administration of a test ensures that factors associated with the testing environment are the same across test takers.

Another way to promote reliability is to use clear scoring rules—such as objectively scored items. If subjectively scored items are desirable, then training raters how to use a rubric to guide their evaluations would be one approach to improve score reliability. Rater effects occur when factors associated with the rater (fatigue, personal views/bias) affect their judgment on the performance they are evaluating, such as a student's oral communication skills. When there are multiple raters, it is important that raters are normed with each other. This is called inter-rater reliability.

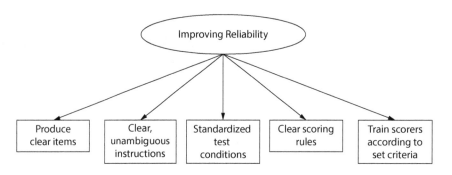

FIGURE 8.12 IMPROVING RELIABILITY

Reliability deals with score consistency of scores and is a prerequisite for validity, which deals with whether scores reflect the trait they were designed to measure. Thus, reliability is a necessary, but not sufficient condition for validity.

There has been a lot written about factors of validity and reliability. A good source is Campbell and Stanley (2010), *Experimental and Quasi-Experimental Designs for Research*.

Survey Research

Probably the most widely used type of research design in social sciences is the survey. Surveys provide a series of closed-ended questions and can be administered to large groups of people.

The way the questions are stated can demonstrate relationships between variables. Surveys can be designed to answer a variety of interactions between variables. There is an art to survey research because the response rate is usually low. To obtain reliability and validity to the data, the response rate is critical.

A quick perusal of empirical articles in many social science journals will illustrate how widespread researcher-developed surveys play in the source of data to be analyzed for publication. These range everywhere from motivation, self-efficacy, empowerment, job satisfaction, or academic achievement. I will use the terms tests, surveys, and questionnaires interchangeably, as they are all devices used to collect data on one or more study participants. Well-known instruments include IQ tests to measure intelligence, the Graduate Record Exam to measure aptitude at the graduate level, and the Beck's Depression Inventory to measure depression. As evident here and in our daily practice, the use of instruments across social science, educational, clinical, and vocational contexts is widespread. Scores derived from these measures are used for a host of decision-making purposes, such as program planning, placement, and/or certification.

The instruments used across contexts differ in terms of various factors, such as whether the scale is objectively or subjectively scored. Objectively scored instruments are those that include response options that can be used to unambiguously assign a respondent to a particular location along the continuum of the measured trait. For example, a self-report motivation survey based on a Likert response scale (1 = Strongly Disagree to 5 = Strongly Agree) is objective because two different raters can independently observe which response option was selected across a given item set. That is, the respondent circled "Strongly Disagree" for Item 1, "Disagree" for Item 2, and so on. Similarly, a multiple-choice test is objective when the response options include correct/incorrect answers.

Achievement tests provide excellent examples of objectively scored tests. Typically, examinees mark their response to the item by selecting one multiple-choice answer, which is then recorded as correct or incorrect. Items scored as correct/incorrect are referred to as dichotomously scored items, because there is only one of two ways in which the examinee performed on the item: they either got it right or wrong.

On the other hand, subjectively scored instruments are those that do not have an absolute correct response. These include essay questions, where scoring is more subjective—when one rater assigns a score based on punctuation and grammar and another rater based a score on presented ideas.

There is an important difference between measuring across the physical and behavioral sciences. Within the physical sciences, the repeated measurement of something (table, book) will result in the same outcome (weight, height). On the other hand, in the behavioral sciences, the repeated measurement of the same individual's intelligence, academic achievement, motivation, etc., is susceptible to change and will fluctuate based on the group of individuals in which data was obtained (changes between samples gathered from the population). Further, whereas we can be afforded the luxury to measure the height of a table a number of times in a given time frame (five times within ten minutes, every other day, etc.), within social science research, we may only have one opportunity (perhaps two at best) to collect data on a given sample (e.g., students, clients, parents).

Thus, the inferences drawn from the physical sciences can often be based on one observation. In the behavioral sciences (e.g., social work, education, counseling), it is necessary to collect information on a group of individuals (sample) to make inferences about a larger group of individuals (population). As previously discussed, because individuals differ in so many different ways, it is often necessary to collect information on a large group to generalize the results to the larger population.

Uses of survey/test scores include prediction (investigating whether motivation is related to academic achievement), summative (determining what concepts students have learned to date), placement (using academic achievement scores to recommend after-school program participation), and program evaluation (determining whether a program is meeting its desired end), among many. Within social science research, scores are also used to judge the relationship between the independent and dependent variables, or determine the efficacy of a given instruction, for example.

Educational, clinical, and vocational tests can also be classified based on the use of obtained scores. In particular, the ways in which information from scores are to be used provide a basis to classify a test as norm- or criterion-referenced. A norm-referenced test is any one designed to yield scores to rank or compare individuals to similar age/grade peers. This typically includes the individually administered, standardized tests, such as the Woodcock Johnson Tests of Achievement, Peabody Picture Vocabulary, and SATs/GREs, among others.

As has been discussed, the survey development within social science contexts is designed to provide an operational measure of a construct of interest, such as: quality of life, teacher collaboration, anxiety, leadership, and so on. As such, the items that comprise the measure are generated to directly correspond with the underlying construct. The relationship between individual scale items and the underlying construct. For example, the instrument is comprised of twenty items that ask about an individual's level of motivation to perform a given task. Responses are provided on a Likert scale: Strongly Disagree to Strongly Agree. There are multiple questions that relate to the same topic, but as a test for reliability, they are spread throughout the twenty questions rather than all lumped together. Since there is only one motivation score that is being developed for each respondent, then how the respondent answers each of the questions will be tabulated for a score developed for each respondent based on an average score of the related items. This instrument can be empirically tested to determine whether the twenty items actually measure just one underlying factor or if other factors may be present. The statistical analysis used to examine this is called factor analysis.

Steps to Survey Development

There are three options to consider when deciding to use a survey in research, which are: develop an instrument from scratch, adapt a pre-existing instrument, or use a pre-existing instrument. The option to choose depends on several factors. One factor is whether or not a pre-existing instrument is available to measure the construct of interest. Another factor is whether or not a pre-existing instrument is relevant for the intended audience. For example, it is unlikely a measure of motivation designed for college students will be an appropriate measure for worker motivation to stay in a public child welfare position.

Thus, when developing an instrument, several factors need to be considered. First, the purpose(s) of the instrument need to be determined, such as: what is it designed to measure, who will complete it, and how will scores be used. Typically, the purpose of developing an instrument in social science research is to measure the independent and dependent variables.

Second, the target population must be identified. This is important because the items comprising the instrument must be at an appropriate reading level and be able to measure what the instrument was designed to measure.

Third, questions comprising the instrument must be relevant, clear, and easily readable. Also, one must consider whether the items will be closed-ended, where the person completing the instrument must select a response option (e.g., Likert scale), or open-ended, where the respondent is free to express any response to the question.

Fourth, prior to administering the instrument to the target population (e.g., sample), it is a good idea to pilot-test the instrument by administering it to a group of individuals that represent the target population. Typically, pilot-testing of an instrument is done on a representative sample of twenty-five to fifty individuals. The aim of pilot-testing an instrument is to determine whether the items are clear, if the instrument is too long, inspecting item statistics (e.g., item mean, standard deviation), or if the instrument does not measure the trait it was designed for.

Other factors to consider are selecting a sample using an appropriate sampling technique, such as those discussed in the next chapter. In quantitative studies, larger samples are desired, as they are more likely to represent the larger population. Invitation to participate in a study is routinely done by using a cover letter describing the study purpose and identifying what study participation entails. This includes explaining the purpose of the survey (or why data is being collected), ensuring potential participants that all information will be confidential and anonymous, who is supporting or conducting the research, how the results will be used, and when to return the survey if they decide to participate. Hence, the cover letter serves a vital role in social science research, as it is the vehicle to encourage study participation. These are all elements that the Institutional Review Board (IRB) will want to have addressed. Discussion about IRB will be in two chapters.

Ideally, one wants to invite more individuals to be in a study than will be needed. This is because surveys usually only generate about a 15 percent response rate. There is the Dillman (1972) technique that has been developed in order to maximize survey responses. More on the Dillman technique a little later.

Once the survey and cover letter have been approved by the IRB and finalized, the next step entails sending it to your potential sample. It is not uncommon to have a response rate equal to or less than 20 percent, so it is advisable to recruit as many people as possible to ensure a representative sample in which to collect data. Based on the fact that not everyone will participate in a study, a plan for non-responses, such as the Dillman (1979) technique, should be made.

What Dillman (1979) proposed was sending out a series of surveys to help improve the response. He suggests sending it out the first time and then a week later sending out a follow-up postcard reminding recipients to complete the survey. Two weeks later, a second copy of the survey is sent to those who have not responded. Two weeks following that, the survey is sent one more time via certified mail with a prepaid return receipt envelope. This technique has been modified for online surveys, which is one reason that there are times when it seems your inbox is bombarded with reminders to complete a survey. Using the Dillman (1979) technique should generate at least a 65 percent response rate for your survey, which is an acceptable rate.

Once the instruments have been completed, data analysis is conducted to determine (a) characteristics of the sample (males/females, average age, etc.), (b) whether group differences on the dependent variable were observed, or (c) if two variables are related or not. Last, the results of the study are written up for dissemination—master's paper, dissertation, publication.

Designing Questions

The items that comprise a survey should be as clear as possible and reflect the characteristics of the construct one is seeking to measure. Five characteristics of good items to comprise an instrument include:

1. Questions should be clear and understood by all respondents
   a. age/grade appropriate
   b. not induce stress/anxiety
2. Questions need to be administered or communicated to respondents
   a. Pencil-paper/electronic format
3. What constitutes an adequate answer should be communicated clearly
   a. Provide instructions to ensure respondents know how to respond to each item, such as circling response option on a Likert scale (circle): Strongly Disagree, Disagree, Agree, Strongly Agree
4. Unless measuring knowledge is the goal of the question, all respondents should have access to the information needed to answer the question accurately
   a. All respondents completing the survey should have something in common—immersed in study context (school, clinic), similar background/diagnosis/grade level, job, etc.
5. Respondents must be willing to provide the answers called for in the question
   a. Ensure confidentiality, item clarity, reduce social desirability

Here is a consideration of factors to developing clear, unambiguous items to measure factual information. As with any question, words should be clear and not be ambiguous; also, key terms should be defined. For example, if you seek to measure extracurricular involvement, you may want to provide a definition of extracurricular so that those completing the instrument will have the same understanding of the term as you intended.

Second, minimize the difficulty of recall and reporting tasks. Here, instead of asking individuals about how long they engaged in a particular activity last week, perhaps ask them "on average" how long they engage in an activity—such as going to the gym. Or, if you seek to understand how individuals felt over a length of time, indicate this in the item, such as: "In the past three days, have you felt disconnected from those around you?"

Third, for objectives that pose special definitional or are recall challenges, use multiple questions.

Fourth, provide respondents help with recall and place events in time by encouraging the use of association and other memory aids.

Fifth, make sure the form of the answer given fits the reality to be described—such as one's perceived impact of participating in a given intervention.

Sixth, keep the questions simple. Do not use complex or compound questions. Either/or questions can be confusing in how to respond; therefore, it is better to make two or more questions out of that particular item.

Last, design all aspects of the data collection to minimize the possibility that any respondent will feel his or her interests will be best served by giving an incorrect answer to a question. That is, pose questions that will not make the respondent not be truthful, such as: involvement in gangs, drug/alcohol use, etc.

Evaluating Questions

Once items are developed, the next step involves evaluating item quality. Several approaches are provided here. First, focus group discussions with those with a level of expertise on the measured trait can be used to ensure the clarity and applicability of questions, such as interviewing participants from the pilot study who have similar backgrounds to the participants that you are seeking to study. Second, cognitive interviews can be used. Here, individuals are presented with the questions and asked to discuss their process and thoughts as they evaluate how they would respond to a set of questions.

Another approach is to field-test the questions (pilot study) on a representative group of individuals that reflect your target population. The aim of pilot-testing items is to examine if items are clear, how long it takes to complete the instrument, and to judge whether certain items need to be deleted/modified/replaced. Also, a statistical analysis of the questions could be used once a subset of data has been collected. Here, the measures of central tendency and variability could be used to see if an item is too easy/difficult and whether or not those who completed the questions were more similar or different in their responses, as based on the standard deviation.

A unique approach is to administer the items using alternative wording, based on the same idea, to see if respondents provide different answers. If so, the question may be confusing.

Last, the same instrument could be administered to the same group of individuals at two different time points (three-week interval) to investigate the consistency of their answers.

Although survey studies seem to be the most popular type of design, there are other designs where there is no interaction with client systems. This can be in the form of historical designs that look at information. This could be either a qualitative or a quantitative study in that you are looking at secondary information that already exists, but you are analyzing it based on specific questions that you want answered. For example, I began the homeless shelter study by looking at case records of shelter guests to determine the nature of the information gathered to see how it contributed to the relationship between the shelter, the staff, and the guest. This would be a type of historical design that could be used.

Action Research

To this point, the designs have been focusing on research for hypothesis testing. Hypothesis testing is the most common way that social scientists conduct research as it relates to thesis development, dissertation work, or publications. However, it does not fully relate to decision-making or more practical applications of the research process.

There are a number of research methods that focus on research for the purpose of making a decision or to provide information that will lead to an action. The large umbrella for research leading to action is called action research that was developed by Kurt Lewin in the 1940s. Subsequent to Lewin's utilization of the term, there have been a number of other terms applied, all with a similar focus: to gather data that will be used to inform a decision. More recently, the terms being used are participatory action research (PAR) (Lawson, Caringi, Pyles, Jurkowski, and Bozlak, 2015) and community-based participatory research (CBPR) (Hacker, 2013). Both PAR and CBPR provide a framework where the research is conducted for action (gather data for understanding); research is conducted in action (monitoring how the use of data can affect a change); and research conducted on action (using the data to evaluate the effect of the change as a result of the action being taken).

Action research has been used to address inequalities in society in order to create some level of change. In the 1980s, Paulo Freire engaged oppressed populations in Brazil using action research to improve some of their living conditions. He coined the term Emancipatory Praxis since he saw the research as being a way to address societal inequalities.

Recently, I have been using CBPR as a way to address inequalities in our community and involve it in the decision-making process to support a change. As such, we have first had to define the community through a community mapping process and then conduct a power analysis to ascertain the decision-makers affecting the community. Then, we provide data to the community to support a change perspective that is relevant to the population being served. Although we continue to use quantitative and qualitative measures to collect and analyze data, there is a deeper meaning to the data, as it is used for making decisions that affect the community. In addition, it is the community that is making the decisions, and as such, the data has become a powerful tool in the decision-making process.

Just as in traditional research, there are a number of steps to action research. I will not be going into detail in this volume, but it is an important concept in designing your research study to ask the question, "Who is this for?" If there is a specific community that can be targeted and you are willing to work with it, then make a determination if a form of action research is the type that you would like to conduct.

Thus, a research design is simply a plan of how you are going to collect your data. This is an important part of the information that you will be sending to the IRB for review, as the IRB has the responsibility for protecting human subjects. Thus, whatever design you choose, it will still need to be reviewed and approved by a number of objective individuals who will be making sure that you are not violating any human rights. More on the IRB process in two chapters.

SELECTING THE RESEARCH DESIGN

The design of the study refers to the way in which relationships are to be studied. Choices among designs will always require compromises between the practical and the ideal. Well-designed research, like anything else designed well, should be more efficient and better suited to your needs than a haphazard approach. Poorly designed research may be inefficient or, even worse, may make it impossible for you to analyze the data legitimately!

Determine, in general, what kind of design is most practical and suitable for your study. Choose a design, describe its structure, and then discuss the pros and cons of the design you selected. But first, state your hypothesis.

_____

_____

Select a research design (quasi-experimental, survey, single subject, historical, other).

_____

Describe the structure of the design (if it is easier to diagram the design, then do so on the back).

_____

_____

_____

Discuss the pros and cons of the design.

_____

_____

_____

Address how the design is addressing issues of internal and external validity.

_____

_____

_____

Sampling

Since the general aim of research is to broaden our understanding of a given phenomenon of interest, regardless of the question at hand, a decision has to be made on whom to collect and analyze data to address the question. Ideally, it would be best to study the entire population, but that is not realistic; therefore, it is important to select a portion of the population that hopefully represents the entire population.

The population can be defined as the larger group that one seeks to learn about. In understanding what homeless shelters do to address the problems of homelessness, the population of interest ranged from homeless people to shelters to a number of ancillary services addressing the needs of homeless people. Even within these ranges, there were sub-samples such as the differences between single adult shelters and family shelters, street homeless people and couch-surfing homeless people, etc. As should be evident, if one was interested in studying characteristics of these groups or their response to interventions, it would be difficult, if not impossible, to collect data on all individuals comprising the population of interest. This is because the population(s) of interest may consist of perhaps thousands or millions of people. Such factors as resources, time, and cost will prevent us the opportunity to collect the information on all members of the population. Instead, it is more feasible to select a representative sub-group from the population to collect data from to learn about the population.

The sample is a group or individual(s) selected from the larger population to collect data to address the research question(s). The use of samples in research is advantageous because it affords the opportunity to learn about the population based on data collected on a more manageable number of individuals or groups.

As to be discussed, there are many approaches to selecting a sample from a population. The most important factor, however, is ensuring that proper methods are used to select the sample so that the collected data can be considered reliable, credible, and valid, among others. The aim of research is to conduct a non-biased investigation into a specific research question. The graphic below provides a visual illustration of the steps involved in moving from a population of interest, or the group one wants to learn more about, to the selection and attainment of a sample of participants to collect data. The left side of the illustration encompasses the factors that must be considered by the researcher when deciding on sample selection. First, one must consider "Who do you want to generalize to?" This deals with what group of people in the population you want to learn something about—what is the issue that needs to be addressed for this group? For example, if one is interested in promoting strategies to help children under the age of ten cope with divorce, the population is children under the age of ten dealing with issues related to their parents' divorce.

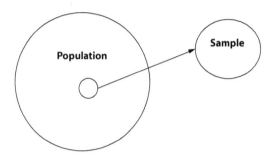

FIGURE 9.1 SAMPLE & POPULATION

The second issue is "What population do you have access to?" This issue deals with feasibility—on who can you gain access to collect data? If you are situated in California's Central Valley, then it is most feasible to find children under the age of ten dealing with divorce in this area. Although it may serve useful to collect data on these children in other states or California counties, you may not have the time or resources to collect this data. Instead, it may be more feasible to collect data from children in local school or clinical settings.

The third issue is "How can you get access to them?" Again, this is a feasibility issue. If you work within a school setting, you may seek to recruit study participants by working with the counseling center or with students that you already know. Perhaps there is a support group for children whose parents are going through a divorce. These are logical avenues to recruit children under the age of ten to be a part of your inquiry. Largely, this component deals with the time and resources available to obtain data on the sample.

Last, "Who is in your study?" addresses those that are actually recruited and retained as part of the study. These are the individuals in whom data will be collected and analyzed, with decisions and recommendations to be based.

Quantitative Sampling Techniques

Key Sampling Concepts

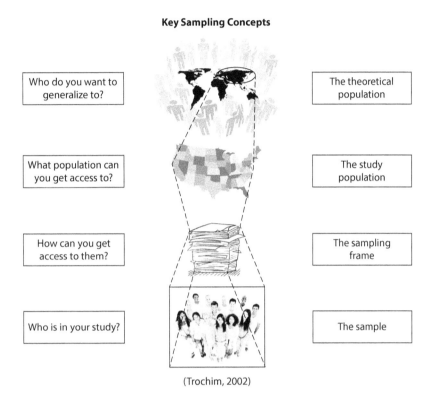

(Trochim, 2002)

FIGURE 9.2 KEY SAMPLING CONCEPTS

The right side of the figure shows the actual steps one takes to select a sample from the population. As shown, these steps are aligned with the questions one must address on the left side of the figure. Thus, the Theoretical Population includes individuals one seeks to study or learn more about.

The Study Population, on the other hand, are those individuals that one may have access to, such as all children under the age of ten in one's own school district. Here, the study population only includes those individuals that the researcher actually has access to.

The Sampling Framework addresses the strategy used to select individuals from the population into the study. As to be discussed, there are several approaches within quantitative and qualitative research to selecting study participants to comprise the sample. The method of sample selection should be explicit in the articles you read and something to pay close attention to.

Last, the Sample is the population sub-group who are actually the participants in the study. Thus, if a study sought to test an intervention to address the problems of ten-year-old children whose parents have divorced (with an unknown population of perhaps thousands of children) where the data is based on a sample of fifty students, a critical question is whether the sample is representative of the population. Unless the sample reflects the population, it is reasonable to ask, "How likely are the study findings generalized to the entire population?" This issue will be discussed below.

The reality is that it is unlikely that we would be able to study an entire population. Thus, the selection of a sample, particularly one that is representative of the population, is important for the findings to be considered useful.

Deciding on a sample is dependent upon whether your research question is quantitative or qualitative and how that particular methodology will be used in your design. Both quantitative and qualitative methodologies seek the use of strategic methods to address a given question, but they differ in terms of the methods used to gather the data to address the research question.

Quantitative research seeks to use data collected on a sample to make inferences (inferential statistics will be described in chapter 11) about the population. This entails the use of statistical inference, or probability statements to make judgments about the likelihood of a given outcome occurring in the population, given its observation based on a sample. In quantitative research, values of the sample, such as mean and standard deviation, are used to estimate similar values in the population. For example, given a large, representative sample, the sample mean can be used to estimate the population mean. The identified sample mean is called a statistic, and includes measures of central tendency and variability. Notably, sample statistics can change each time they are estimated based on a different sample. This is because each sample drawn from the population may differ from sample to sample due to random variation.

On the other hand, the values of the population are called parameters. Thus, the population mean, median, mode, variance, and standard deviation are parameters. They are parameters because they do not change. That is, if one was to estimate the mean from the entire population, it would always be the same over repeated estimations, because information collected on all the individuals in the population were used. Within quantitative research, large samples are desired, typically over thirty individuals or higher, perhaps even 1,000+ individuals. The two approaches to sampling in quantitative research include probability and non-probability sampling.

In qualitative research, the sample is selected for a particular purpose. Largely, this is to begin to gain an in-depth understanding about a particular phenomenon. Ubiquitous to qualitative research is the use of small sample sizes, perhaps even one. This is because one is looking to begin to understand a phenomenon about a particular situation that could be generalized later once the parameters are identified. Although Glaser and Strauss (1967) might say to continue collecting data until you reach data saturation, that is usually not realistic. Thus, Cheek (2011) describes sample sizes in qualitative research as a set of trade-offs of what is feasible. Instead, the aim is to select individuals or cases that will yield rich data to understand the phenomenon of interest. The sampling approach used in qualitative research is more of a purposeful sampling.

Here are some sampling strategies that can be considered in quantitative research. This flowchart illustrates that they can be grouped according to whether the approach falls under a probability or non-probability sampling approach.

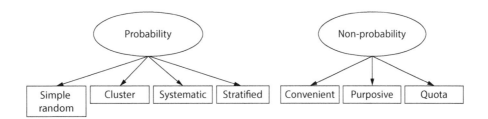

FIGURE 9.3 QUANTITATIVE SAMPLING TECHNIQUES

A probability sample is one in which each element, or individual, of the population has a known non-zero probability of selection into the sample. Simply stated, "each individual within the population has some chance (or probability) of being selected into the sample." Probability sampling techniques include simple random sampling, cluster sampling, and systematic sampling.

Non-probability sampling procedures are those that do not provide the opportunity of each population member to be included in the sample. Thus, not all population members have an equal chance of being included in the sample, for whatever reason (e.g., difficult to access). Non- probability sampling techniques include convenient, purposive, and quota sampling.

Probability sampling is advantageous because it seeks to eliminate any experimenter bias in the selection of a sample. This is because, as stated, each element (or individual) has a known non-zero probability of selection. More simply, each individual in the population has some likelihood of being selected into the sample. Therefore, only when each individual has a chance of being in the sample is it a probability sample technique, and it is not a probability sample if probabilities of selection are not known.

Random Sampling

The first probability sampling approach is simple random sampling. Within this approach, the only focus is obtaining a random sample from the population. For example, say the population of interest was at-risk ninth-grade students (perhaps 2,000 students) within a given geographic area, and the desired sample size was one hundred. At the most basic level, each of the 2,000 students could be assigned a random number from one to 2,000. Then, if we sorted their random numbers in ascending order, the first one-hundred students in this list would comprise the sample. Notably, the simple random sampling approach is only concerned with randomly selecting individuals from the population. It is not concerned with ensuring that the sample is representative of the population in terms of potentially relevant demographics—such as gender, race/ethnicity, SES, parent education level, etc. A simple random sample is most readily useable when the target population consists of individuals (e.g., students, patients) within a given institution, such as school district, hospital, or specific geographic location. Or, when there is clear knowledge of all the individuals comprising the population.

Stratified Random Sampling

Whereas simple random sampling is only concerned with selecting individuals from the population to be included into the sample, it does not consider ensuring representative population sub-groups. The stratified random sampling procedure addresses this by breaking the population into relevant sub-groups, say in terms of gender, race/ethnicity, grade level, etc., and then randomly selecting individuals within these sub-groups to comprise the sample. Thus, this approach provides an approach to selecting a sample from the population that considers the various population sub-groups.

The following steps indicate the procedure for employing a stratified random sampling approach. First, the population is divided into the various population sub-groups of interest, such as gender, race/ethnicity, age group, marital status, etc. Importantly, the population is only divided into those sub-groups of most relevance to the research. Thus, for example, if one was interested in investigating factors associated with suspension/expulsion practices, one's sample should include representative numbers of male and female (as well as race/ethnicity) found in the population. As such, the basis for grouping must be known prior to sample selection. Once the population has been divided, the last step is selecting a random sample of individuals from each of the sub- groups. Sampling from population sub-groups can be based on the use of simple random sampling—just selecting, for example, one hundred individuals from each sub-group to comprise the sample or by proportionally selecting from the sub-groups based upon the representation of the sub-group within the larger population. Stratified random sampling is important to consider when there are known population sub-groups with known differences, such as language, culture, or socioeconomic status.

Cluster Random Sampling

Cluster random sampling applies when investigating a group of individuals with some shared characteristic (e.g., attend same school or clinic). In this sampling approach, sampling occurs at the group level, as opposed to the individual (or case) level, which occurred for simple random and stratified random sampling. That is, cluster random sampling entails the random selection of groups (e.g., schools, clinics, job sites) so that individuals comprising this group are all included in the sample. For example, say the research question was based on investigating the effects of Positive Behavior Supports and Interventions (PBIS) on students' academic achievement and behavior (e.g., suspension/expulsion) in California. In this instance, it is not feasible to randomly pull students out of their respective schools across the state and put them into a different school with the program. Instead, it would be more feasible to randomly select, say, ten schools across the state to see whether those schools exposed to PBIS demonstrate increased gains in academic achievement and decreases in undesirable behaviors than comparable schools without the program. As such, instead of sampling at the individual level, sampling occurs at the school level. Here, the schools represent the cluster of students who will be exposed to one of the treatment conditions—PBIS (treatment group) or no PBIS (control group).

As stated here, cluster sampling is conducted by randomly selecting a given cluster of individuals (high school students) from the target population (all high school students). This cluster of individuals serves to represent the population. Typically, the population is divided into groups, such as geographic (e.g., rural and urban schools or clients) or organization (schools, programs). This sampling approach is most commonly used for investigations into the effects of small- and large-scale programs (e.g., after-school or treatment modalities) commonly situated within educational or clinical settings.

Systematic Random Sampling

Systematic sampling is another type of probability sampling technique. In this approach, the target population is identified and put in some type of order (based on last name, zip code, etc.). Then, individuals are selected into the population based on a straightforward manner based on the following algorithm. As stated, first the population is put in some type of order.

As an example, say a car dealership seeks to inquire into customer satisfaction among all new car buyers over the past year (perhaps 3,000 individuals—the target population). Say the car dealership only has enough time and resources to collect data on 500 individuals (the sample). To attain this sample size, a sampling interval is estimated based on N (population size = 3,000), the sample size (n = 500), and the sampling interval of 6 (6 = 3,000/500). Thus, if the 3,000 individuals who purchased a car within the last year are ordered based on some criteria (time since they bought the car), the sample is obtained by randomly selecting the first individual to be in the sample (person 6), and an interval of 6 would select subsequent individuals to be in the sample. In this example, then, beginning with person 6, the next study recruit would be person 12, then person 18, then person 24, then person 30, and so on until 500 individuals have been identified.

Non-Probability [Non-Random] Sampling

Whereas probability sampling procedures offer the luxury of providing all members of the population some likelihood of being selected into the sample, non-probability sampling techniques are also commonly used. The distinguishing feature of these methods is that they do not offer all population members equal likelihood of being selected into the sample. Due to various factors, these sampling approaches are among the most commonly used in social science, clinical, and vocational research since researchers do not always have ready access to the target population. Typically, we only have access to a portion of the target population, called the accessible population.

For example, a researcher may be interested in investigating strategies to promote the behavioral and academic outcomes of autistic children, and the target population is all students with autism in the U.S. However, the researcher may reside in California's Central Valley. Restrictions related to time, funding, and resources may seriously impede the researcher's ability to implement and test the effectiveness of a particular instructional strategy for all these students in the U.S. population. Instead, it is thus more feasible for the researcher to concentrate his/her efforts on those students with autism attending schools in the immediate area. As this example illustrates, this is a common scenario that faces researchers in the social sciences and, consequently, results in non-probability sampling techniques being a routinely used sampling approach.

Convenient Sampling

Convenient sampling is probably one of the most commonly used non-probability sampling techniques. This approach entails the selection of a sample due to the researcher's access to the participants (e.g., students in local school, patients attending outpatient clinic, individuals in college program). In this case, the sample may not be tied to the purposes of the research; instead, they serve the purpose of providing data to address one's research question. A convenient sample may consist of teachers/students within your school, clients receiving rehab services, or individuals enrolling for unemployment. The common thread here is that the sample was selected from the population because one had easy access to them.

Purposive Sampling

Purposive sampling is another type of non-probability sampling technique based on intentionally selecting individuals to be part of a study because they are linked to the purposes of the research. Purposive sampling would be appropriate if one was interested in studying the effects of a behavioral modification technique on a low-incident population (e.g., third-grade autistic students). Here, the researcher would intentionally seek out individuals who met this criterion, or have characteristics in which the researcher is interested in learning more about, since the research question is based on this population. As such, purposive sampling is leveled at selecting a sample from a "hard-to-get population," or one that occurs less frequently than is common in the population. In general, purposive sampling is used with low-incident populations that consist of less than thirty individuals.

Quota Sampling

Quota sampling represents the final type of non-probability sampling technique we will consider. Quota sampling is aligned with the stratified random sampling technique discussed earlier. However, instead of each individual within the population sub-groups (e.g., gender, race/ethnicity) having an equal chance of selection, individuals are selected based on their accessibility. That is, quota sampling seeks to include representative population sub-groups in the sample, but individuals in the sub-group do not have equal likelihood of selection into the sample. For example, say for accreditation purposes your program wanted to survey the satisfaction of 400 graduates regarding the applicability of the content taught in the program to their actual job experience. Based on a quota sampling approach, the program could select one-hundred students within each concentration/specialization content area within the curriculum. This sample could be further broken down to select certain numbers of males/females and/or racial/ethnic groups within the graduates from the program.

The initial approach to sampling represents a logic to define your particular part of the universe that will appropriately answer your question. Again, the larger your sample, the more data you will have relating to your question, but is that realistic? There are costs—money, time, and resources—associated with collecting data from a sample. In addition, there is also the accessibility question to consider. To be realistic means to take these factors into consideration and select a sample size that is manageable and doable given the resources available for your study. If you are a single researcher, identify a sample size that you can manage in your life.

Qualitative Sampling

The basis of qualitative research is to gain a rich, in-depth perspective regarding a particular question at hand. The data collected typically involve interviews, focus groups, direct observation, and documents. Thus, unlike quantitative research, the data used in qualitative research lends itself to being collected on a select number of cases or groups, not a large sample like that used in quantitative research. Many times, the size of the sample is determined by what the researcher feels s/he can handle. For example, Glaser and Strauss (1967) talk about data saturation in developing grounded theory; however, it is not realistic that a researcher will be able to continue collecting data until saturation is achieved and still get it done in a reasonable time.

As a result, qualitative sampling techniques use a purposive sampling approach. That is, individuals or groups are selected into the study for a purpose, typically to gain rich information of the phenomenon at hand. This type of sampling approach is also called judgment sampling. Examples include extreme case or snowball/chain sampling. Similar to quantitative research, there are a host of qualitative sampling techniques. Many examples are listed here, including: comprehensive, maximum variation, extreme case, typical case, homogeneous, and snowball or chain sampling. Each sampling approach has its own approach to selecting individuals or groups into a sample. Collectively, they share the feature of seeking to identify individuals or groups into the sample because they possess characteristics that will foster an understanding of the question under investigation.

Extreme, or deviant, case sampling entails the selection of individuals to a study because they possess some unique characteristic or quality of relevance to the study's research question(s). More specifically, the individual(s) of interest possess a unique trait from which you, as the researcher, can learn that may not be available through other sources.

For example, say a qualitative researcher was interested in factors associated with resilience among students in poverty and the attainment of a high school diploma. An extreme case sampling approach would entail selecting students with very high levels of poverty, such as students identified as homeless or a certain threshold below the federal poverty line. As another example, if the focus was on the impact of gambling on life outcomes (e.g., marriage, employment), extreme case may entail seeking to recruit one or more individuals into the sample who have lost everything to gambling (e.g., job, marriage) and are now homeless.

Maximum variation (or heterogeneity) sampling is another type of approach to sampling in qualitative research. This approach is based on the selection of individuals, or cases, that relate to the study research question but have diverse characteristics or traits, such as belief systems, race/ethnicity, geographic location, and position in various organizations (administrator, worker), among others. The aim of selecting individuals with diverse backgrounds and experiences is to identify common themes in the data collected from individuals that differ in important ways. In particular, there are two types of findings to be gained from maximum variation sampling: (a) rich descriptions of each case, or uniqueness, and (b) information on themes shared across different individuals or cases. For example, when trying to identify what happens in a homeless shelter to address the needs of people who were homeless, it was important to include the perspectives of both the recipients of the services (homeless guests) and the people administering the services (staff). In this case, the variation occurs with the selection of individuals who differ in terms of their role in the shelter. The aim would be to compare the information obtained across the population sub-groups to examine whether their shared views toward addressing homelessness were consistent to the needs.

Other qualitative sampling techniques include intensity, homogeneous, and typical case sampling. **Intensity sampling** entails the identification and selection of individuals who represent the phenomenon of interest intensely. For example, a qualitative investigation into the effects of depression on marital satisfaction may seek to sample individuals with clinical depression and have extreme marital difficulties attributed to the manifestation of an individual's depression. Another example could be the educational experiences of rural students in a low-income school. In this case, sampling would seek to identify and recruit students in a rural community who experience high levels of poverty. In this case, these individuals have a high intensity of the characteristics of interest, including: depression, married, resides in rural community, and in poverty. As these examples illustrate, prior information is needed to intelligently select the sample within this framework.

Homogeneous sampling is based on the selection of individuals based on their similarity, or part of the same population sub-group of interest (e.g., sex, race/ethnicity, intervention program, clinic). Homogeneous sampling is most commonly used when the research seeks to learn something about a particular population sub-group, so it is important to sample individuals from that group or with shared characteristics.

Typical case sampling is used to identify and select individuals from a particular group or culture that are "typical" in nature; that is, the cases possess no major uniqueness. This is typically conducted through the use of key informants familiar with the target population to identify potential recruits for the sample. Typical case sampling would occur if a qualitative study sought to investigate worker involvement in the development and methods to sustain a professional learning community to promote worker and agency outcomes. Here, the researcher could rely on the input of executive directors to identify workers to collect data. It would be of interest to collect data about workers who are typical, or have no unique characteristics (e.g., negative beliefs, first-year employees).

Snowball or chain sampling is another type of qualitative sampling technique that relies on the recommendations of key informants to identify individuals with specific characteristics of interest to participate in a study. Snowball sampling could be illustrated by a researcher who sought to investigate the effect of a particular learning strategy on students with disabilities. In this case, snowball sampling would occur when the researcher located a school utilizing the particular strategy and then asked the school to identify another school using the same strategy. Here, based on the recommendations of key informants, the sample size would grow due to the recommendations of these informants. We have used this technique to identify schools that have been successful in changing their school climate through the use of PBIS. As we identified one district, we asked for referrals to other districts that have adopted the model successfully. A possible downside is that this is not a very diverse view of the application of the model.

Opportunistic or emergent sampling is another type of qualitative sampling approach. In this approach, study participants are selected based on their engagement with the researcher during the course of fieldwork. In this context, the individual under consideration for participation in the sample is unknown prior to the study being conducted. Instead, the decision to include someone in the sample is determined "on the spot" by the researcher. For example, opportunistic sampling would occur if a researcher decided to interview a homeless person who happened to want to share his/her story about factors that contributed to his/her homelessness even though you had met your proposed quota of interviews.

The final qualitative sampling procedure considered is **purposeful random sampling**. Within this sampling approach, a group of individuals or cases that possess the characteristics of interest (e.g., sex, race/ethnicity, participation in program) are identified as a pre-selected number of individuals are randomly selected to participate in the sample. The aim here is to overcome the limitations of potential experimenter bias in the selection of a sample. That is, purposeful random sampling is designed to provide credibility to the sample, not representativeness that deals with generalizing results to population. In this case, if the qualitative question centered on the experiences of homeless people in shelters, the target population, perhaps fifty people, would be all the guests at a participating shelter. Purposeful random sampling would entail randomly sampling perhaps five people from the fifty guests of the shelter.

Thus, where the aim of quantitative research is to generalize results based on a sample to the population, the aim of qualitative research is to gain rich information on a particular sample to understand the phenomenon of interest.

Whereas quantitative research seeks to collect and analyze data obtained from a large, representative sample, the required sample size in qualitative research "depends." That is, it depends on a number of factors: size of target population, data to be collected (interview, observation), costs, time, etc. Patton (2002) reports, "There are no rules for sample size in qualitative inquiry." Therefore, it depends on study purpose, accessibility to target population (or individuals with characteristics of interest), and credibility. Patton provides a strategy for sample size selection in qualitative research. In particular, he advocates the use of "minimum sample," based on the selection of a sample that provides "reasonable coverage" of the event of interest. In this scenario, the researcher builds a case for the proposed sample size, be it one individual to twenty individuals. Thus, if a sample size of five is deemed necessary, the researcher needs to justify this. As such, justification needs to be based on the accuracy of the information to be collected. More specifically, accuracy deals with the degree to which information collected on the sample will yield representative and meaningful information.

As discussed, sampling is the systematic process of identifying and recruiting on one or more individuals to participate in a study, be it a quantitative or qualitative study. Regardless of the methodological approach to the research, a central component is how the sample was identified and obtained. Across studies, it is highly desirable to obtain a sample that will yield accurate and meaningful information to addressing the research question(s) of interest. As evident in published studies, the sampling procedure used may not always be explicated. Consequently, as a person evaluating another's research, it becomes your responsibility to judge the sampling method used and whether this was justified.

The degree to which the sample was obtained ultimately provides the basis for assigning merit to study findings. Thus, a biased sample will not yield information useful for subsequent decision-making purposes. Therefore, it is always critical to examine how a sample in which a study was based was identified and obtained.

Sampling is your best effort in defining a generalizable population that will answer your question. Complete the next two pages as it relates to your study.

SAMPLING

State your hypothesis _____

_____

Is it qualitative or quantitative? _____

What population(s) or source(s) of data will best describe the relationships in your hypothesis?

_____

_____

_____

How do these populations/sources define the relationship beyond your sample? (generalization of results)

_____

_____

_____

Are there differences between your proposed sample and what you would like to have generalized beyond the proposed sample? If yes, revise either or both descriptions to make a better fit.

_____

_____

_____

Describe resource limitations that may affect your sample size.

_____

_____

What is the potential population size? _____

_____

What "sampling frame" will you use? _____

_____

How will you select your sample? _____

_____

_____

_____

What is a realistic sample size? _____

_____

What variables will be controlled for in your sample? _____

_____

Explain any class, race, or gender biases represented by your sample.

_____

_____

How will you address these biases for your study? _____

_____

Describe your final sample. _____

_____

_____

_____

_____

Credits

1. Fig. 9.2: Adapted from William M.K. Trochim's "Key Sampling Concepts."
2. Fig. 9.2a: Copyright © Depositphotos/michaeldb.
3. Fig. 9.2b: Copyright © Depositphotos/tangducminh.
4. Fig. 9.2c: Copyright © Depositphotos/Ihfgraphics.
5. Fig. 9.2d: Copyright © Depositphotos/Rawpixel.

Protection of Human Subjects

Now that we have developed a research design and a sampling frame, it is important to submit your research protocol to the Institutional Review Board or IRB. The rights of human subjects and self-determination in particular should be respected at all times. Thus, even though a person is willing to participate in your research study, it means that the subjects are expecting that there will be no harm as a result of their participation. The goal is to build knowledge and to learn from the subjects.

It is important to understand that even though there are codes of ethics in the social sciences, the United States Government mandated in 1979 that all research needed to be reviewed by an Institutional Review Board (IRB). This evolved following the publishing of the Belmont Report that outlined three basic principles associated with the ethics in regulations governing the use of human subjects in research projects. The three principles are: respect of persons; beneficence; and justice. These will be explained later in this chapter. However, it is also important to understand some basic definitions about how human subjects are defined and how research is defined.

The term human subjects may seem to be self-explanatory; however, it is important to understand that there are no exceptions to the definition. Some of this arose because there were some researchers who chose to study some populations because of convenient access to the population without regard of status. Most of these were conducted prior to the submission of the Belmont Report, which is the reason the report needed to mention them. Such studies as the Tuskegee syphilis study (1932–1972) or the Zimbardo prison study (1971) contributed to a global definition of human subjects to include all living individuals about whom an investigator conducting research obtains data through intervention or interaction and there is identifiable private information about that person.

Then the government needed to define research. Based on the U.S. Government, research is defined as: any systematic investigation designed to develop or contribute to generalizable knowledge. Thus, by looking at the definition of these two terms, it is possible to identify any systematic investigation conducted on any living thing, including animals, would be subject to review by an IRB. Most universities, because they are recipients of federal funding, have IRBs that will review studies on humans and animals.

Thus, in developing your research proposal, plan on having it reviewed by your institution's IRB. This is a safeguard for those participating in the study. In addition, you will not be able to publish the results of your study unless it has gone through the IRB process.

Belmont Report

As previously mentioned, the federal guidelines for human subject research are based on the Belmont Report. There are three components in the Belmont Report: respect for the person; beneficence; and justice. Each will be briefly explained. A full copy of the Belmont Report can be retrieved from: http://www.hhs.gov/ohrp/regulations-and-policy/belmont-report/.

Respect for Person

The Belmont Report describes four aspects as it relates to respect for the person: each person is autonomous; respect privacy; consent for participation; and respect willingness to share confidential information. Thus, a person being autonomous means that each person is an individual and has the right to decide independently whether they will participate or not. When there is a minor, then even the minor has the right to an autonomous decision to participate as well as the parent or guardian of that person. In this case, there is the need for a participant assent as well as consent from the parent or guardian.

Respecting a person's privacy means that every effort needs to be taken to make sure that the information provided by a person participating in a study is kept confidential. This includes everything from the responses being made to contact information. Thus, when reporting interview data, there should not be any information that would be able to identify the individual.

Consent for participation means that every person needs to agree to participate. Even a minor person needs to participate, but because the minor does not have legal jurisdiction, then the minor would complete an assent with the custodial or legal person completing the consent. Thus, there may be the scenario where the legal entity consents but the actual participant does not provide an assent or vice versa. In this instance, the person would not participate in the study.

Finally, the participant in the study needs to be aware that s/he is participating in a study and the intention of the researcher is that the results will be published. In this instance, the participant needs to agree to be willing to share the information provided as a participant in the study.

Beneficence

Simply stated, beneficence is a term that relates to the benefit of the study, or as the Belmont Report states, participation in the study will do no harm to the participant, participation is an opportunity that might benefit the individual, the group the individual represents, or is a benefit to society, and there is minimized risk as a result of participation.

Justice

The third category of the Belmont Report is justice. This is defined as there are no risks placed on any one particular group or another and the benefits of participation will not be exclusive to any particular group. These two aspects mean that the study is conducted in a just and even way.

Although each IRB has an application procedure that you are to follow to apply for review, there are seven federal criteria that relate to all studies. These criteria are:

1. Risks to subjects minimized
2. Risks are reasonable in relation to benefits
3. Selection of subjects is equitable
4. Informed consent—sought and documented
5. Data is monitored to ensure safety of subjects
6. Privacy is protected to maintain confidentiality
7. Protect subjects from coercion or undue influence

Once you feel as though you have satisfied the above criteria, then there are seven questions that you need to ask that will help you prepare for your submission. These seven questions are:

1. Does the study address a significant question?
2. Is the design appropriate?
3. Is the methodology explained?
4. Are response criteria and endpoints identified?
5. Is the sample size appropriate to answer the question?
6. Are data collection and analysis methods adequate?
7. Are early stopping rules adequate, clearly described, and congruent?

All institutions require individuals to complete a training program that provides a history leading to the Belmont Report, description of human subjects, and all the aspects associated with research, including the meanings of beneficence and justice as well as special situations like conducting studies with special populations and under unusual situations. If your institution has not created a training program, the National Institute of Health provides an online training through the Cancer Institute. The URL is: https://phrp.nihtraining.com/users/login.php. Regardless of the training that your institution uses, it is important to download the certificate of completion of the training as evidence that you have completed it.

The questions on the next two pages are standard questions that will help you develop a consent form to be used for your study. If you are doing survey research, a cover letter stating the purpose of the study can suffice for a consent form. It will hold all the information that you want the participant to know to protect them and their anonymity. This will enhance their completion of the survey. So take a few minutes and review the questions and develop your own consent form to protect the people whom you will be studying.

PROTECTION OF HUMAN SUBJECTS

State your hypothesis_____

_____

Whenever humans are the subjects of research, the researcher must consider the following:

A. Describe the potential risks and/or benefits for participating in the study.

_____

_____

_____

_____

B. Describe the subjects and their ability to consent to participate in the research (be particularly aware to protect against coercion). _____

_____

_____

_____

C. How will the subjects be fully informed about the research (including its purposes and risks)? How will you assure that they have freely consented to participate?

_____

_____

_____

_____

D. How will you protect the confidentiality of research data?

_____

_____

_____

E. Write a consent form or cover letter that includes the following elements:

<u>Basic Elements of Informed Consent</u>

1. Statement regarding the research's purpose, expected duration of subject's participation, procedures participants are to follow, and identification of experimental procedures.
2. Description of any foreseeable risks or discomforts to subjects.
3. Description of any benefits to subject or to others that would reasonably be expected.
4. Disclosure of appropriate procedures or treatments.
5. Statement describing how you will maintain confidentiality of the subjects/data.
6. If the research involves more than minimal risk, provide an explanation and type of compensation to be provided if injury occurs.
7. Who to contact for relevant questions about research.
8. Statement that participation is voluntary, refusal or
9. withdrawal will result in no penalty or loss of entitled benefits.

It's all About Relationships—Inferential Statistics

To this point, we have discussed the various types of variables, listing them, developing a research design, and sampling. We have not discussed how to look at the relationship between the variables or how to measure the effect of the independent variable (IV) on the dependent variable (DV). This chapter will provide an understanding of that relationship, some of the ways to measure it, and the statistical tests to determine if there is a significant relationship between the IV and DV. These statistics are called inferential statistics since it infers that there is a statistical relationship between the IV and DV.

Just to recap, data are the pieces of information collected about the variables used to answer your question. To be able to test the relationship between the variables, some type of measurement or numeric representation is used to quantify these variables (this might be different in qualitative research, which will be discussed in the next chapter). These numerical measures are assigned by different tests that relate to the efficacy of the variables. In other words, if one is measuring depression, there are a number of tests that may be used, such as the Beck's Depression Scale or the PHQ-9, that score a numeric value that is used to determine a person's level of depression. In social science research, measurement is the process of assigning a quantitative value to characterize an attribute of an individual or group (e.g., depression, self-efficacy, academic achievement).

This conceptualization of measurement consists of rules for assigning symbols to objects so as to (1) represent quantities of attributes numerically (scaling) or (2) define whether the objects fall in the same or different categories with respect to a given attribute (classification) (Nunnally and Bernstein, 1994, p. 3), or a procedure for the assignment of numbers (scores, measurements) to specified properties of experimental units in such a way as to characterize and preserve specified relationships in the behavioral domain (Lord and Novick, 1968, p. 17).

Data can be collected through specific instruments, observations of behavior, interviews, or any source of information that will be used to define the variables in your study. For example, there are a number of testing measures that will test aspects of behavior. To identify some of the free testing measures, one might look at Corcoran and Fischer (2013), *Measures for Clinical Practice: A Sourcebook, 5th ed.* or Kane and Kane (1981), *Assessing the Elderly: A Practical Guide to Measurement.* These provide some valid and reliable tested measurement tools that you can use to measure different variables.

However, there may not always be instruments for the variables that you are studying. Sometimes you may need to create your own instrument. A survey (discussed in chapter 8) is such an instrument that you develop to measure specific variables for your study. There are other sources of data, such as observations, interviews, or case notes (discussed in chapter 12), that may also be used.

Regardless of the source of the data, once you have the data and want to understand the relationship between the different variables, then you are using inferential statistics as a way to measure the statistical significance between the variables. Just a word of caution here. As discussed in chapter 7, when testing hypotheses, we are not directly testing the relationship, but rather testing the null hypothesis. Thus, with inferential statistics, we are not able to prove whether there is a statistical relationship; rather, the statistics will suggest that there is a relationship or not, which is why it is called inferential statistics and not proof statistics.

Inferential statistics investigates relationships between variables. In general, inferential statistics measures the degree to which selected variables are related, such as reduction of trauma levels following a specific therapeutic treatment, improved skills in relationship to hours spent in professional development, or client outcomes following an intervention. Inferential statistics can measure correlations between variables without actively manipulating variables (IV) and deals with obtaining measures on variables as they naturally occur within the environment, as in a non-experimental design or when the experimenter does manipulate variables in a research study to test for the effect of one variable on another as in an experimental or quasi-experimental design.

Therefore, some of the tests used in inferential statistics include: chi square, T-Test, correlation, regression, multiple regression, ANOVA, discriminate analysis, canonical correlation, and path analysis, just to name a few. Collectively, these designs are based on quantifying the direction and magnitude of the relationship between variables.

Correlations

In its simplest form, inferential statistics focuses on looking at relationships among variables, specifically independent and dependent variables. The most basic type of statistic is using a correlation coefficient to investigate the relationship between two quantitative variables. Specifically, a correlation coefficient provides a numerical index characterizing the magnitude and direction of the relationship between two variables, such as motivation and academic achievement, or perceived quality of relationship with one's counselor and levels of anxiety. Since correlation coefficients reflect the slope of the line of the relationship between two variables as it would be depicted on an X Y graph, the values range from -1 to +1, with values close to zero indicating a weak to no relationship between variables. Values approaching -1 indicate values on one variable increase while they decrease on the other variable. An example of a negative correlation might be the number of days in treatment in relationship to depression levels, or one might hypothesize that the more treatment one receives, the lower the levels of depression.

On the other hand, a correlation coefficient approaching +1 is indicative of a positive relationship between two variables, such as time spent studying and academic achievement—that is, increases in time studying corresponds to higher levels of academic achievement. The finding of a correlation coefficient that falls outside the range of -1 and +1 would indicate a miscalculation. Correlations can be depicted by the following three pictures:

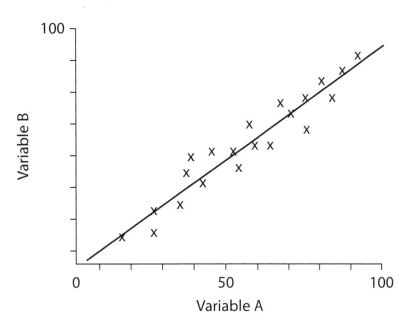

FIGURE 11.1 POSITIVE CORRELATION

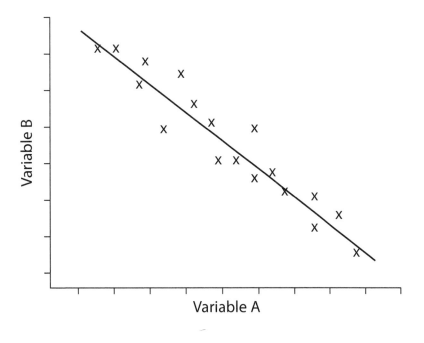

FIGURE 11.2 NEGATIVE CORRELATION

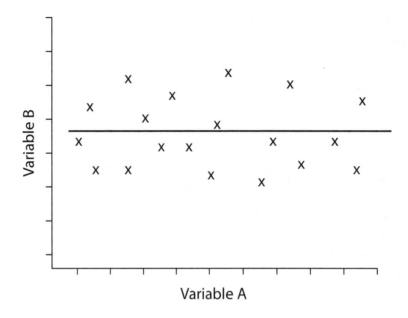

FIGURE 11.3 ZERO CORRELATION

The correlation between variables can be determined for variables with different levels of measurement, such as nominal, ordinal, interval, and ratio. Regardless of the measurement level of the variable(s), correlations are used to describe the relationship between two or more variables. Although there are a variety of correlation types, the three most commonly reported correlations are described. The Pearson Product Moment correlation is used to characterize the relationship between two continuous variables, or those on an interval/ratio level of measurement, such as the scores between two surveys/questionnaires (e.g., anxiety and quality of life, or teacher collaboration and student achievement). Most commonly reported correlation coefficients are based on the Pearson Product Moment correlation, as individuals standing on a measured trait (e.g., depression, leadership) are routinely based on self-report surveys and test scores.

The second type of correlation considered is the Spearman Rho, appropriate for investigating the relationship between two variables on an ordinal level of measurement, such as rank order variables of perceived safety (0 = no sense of safety, 1 = little sense of safety, 3 = general sense of safety, and 4 = complete sense of safety) and level of academic achievement (1 = Far Below, 2 = Below Basic, 3 = Basic, 4 =Proficient, and 5 = Advanced).

Last, the Phi correlation coefficient is useful for characterizing the relationship between two strictly dichotomous variables, such as gender (male, female) and obtained college degree (yes, no). In this context, the Phi coefficient would be used to determine whether a relationship exists between obtaining a college degree and gender, or between gender and high school suspension (yes, no) among high school students. Notably, regardless of the type of correlation coefficient used to describe the relationship between variables, they will always range between -1 and +1 and be interpreted similarly.

Accurate interpretation of the correlation coefficient is important for subsequent decision-making purposes, such as whether the statistical value suggests that there might be value in rejecting the null hypothesis and increasing treatment levels. Since correlation values are symmetrical around zero and range from -1 to +1, they can be interpreted in absolute terms. Thus, a correlation of -.25 and .25 would be "low," just considered in the opposite direction. Thus, a -.25 correlation would indicate a low, negative correlation between two variables, such as time in counseling and anxiety. Although time in counseling may be increasing, anxiety is only decreasing incrementally—perhaps because of other factors above and beyond spending time in counseling. It is typical in social science research to see correlation coefficients range between 0 and |1.00| (the absolute value of 1—either positive or negative), so understanding the way to interpret them is imperative for critically evaluating published research.

Importantly, correlations do not infer causation; instead, they only indicate the association between variables. However, as there are limitations to the inferences that can be drawn from experimental research designs (e.g., quasi-experimental) due to threats to internal/external validity, similar factors should be considered when interpreting correlations. Specifically, to infer an association between variables, three general tenets must be satisfied. First, there is a statistical relationship between the variables, such as time spent in therapy and personal growth. Although an important consideration, a statistical relationship only suggests that there is some systematic variation between the variables—that is, changes are co-occurring across variables, or increased reading is associated with increased spelling and reading fluency skills. However, this does not automatically imply one variable depends on (or causes) the other, or that there is a relationship.

Second, the variable believed to impact the other (e.g., time spent studying) occurs prior to the outcome, or dependent variable (e.g., improved grades). Ideally, the independent variable should be measured prior to the measurement of the dependent variable(s). This is designed to capture the theoretical relationship of the variables, or if one variable occurs (e.g., time spent reading), this influences the outcome of another variable (e.g., improved grades).

Take, for example, a question based on the association between level of professional learning community (PLC) functioning (as measured by scores on a self-report instrument) and college students' academic achievement (as measured by end-of-semester performance). Here, the IV is PLC functioning and the DV is academic achievement, with the target population being college students. To establish a link between PLC engagement and students' academic achievement, one would want to gather the professor data prior to students completing the end-of-semester exam. This is because activities related to PLC functioning should have occurred prior to student testing. It would not make sense to measure PLC functioning after end-of-semester testing.

Last, one must consider whether the correlation between the variables is based on an actual relationship or because of one or more extraneous variables. For example, a moderate correlation found between time spent in one-on-one tutoring in school and academic performance among high-risk students may initially be interpreted that tutoring impacts academic achievement. However, after collecting more data, perhaps it was also found that those receiving one-on-one tutoring were also receiving additional academic support through participation in out-of-class groups. In this case, the relationship between tutoring and achievement may be "spurious" due to the effect of time spent in the out-of-class groups. As with any type of formal experimental design, one must be careful in the identification, selection, and measurement of variables to focus one's study. This is to ensure an accurate evaluation of the problem at hand.

Usually, a correlation between two variables begins by posting all data points on a scatterplot. Within a scatterplot, values of the IV are displayed along the x-axis, while values on the DV are reported on the y-axis. Each "x" in the open space represents the scores for one individual on the independent and dependent variables. Once data has been collected on an adequate number of participants, some overall pattern of the association between variables may (or may not) emerge. It will be a positive correlation between two variables when the slope of the average of the points is a one-to-one relationship, or equivalent to a 45-degree sloped line. A negative correlation would be when the slope of the line is a negative one, or a 135-degree slope. Importantly, a finding of a negative correlation is not a bad thing, and it has equal importance and meaning as a finding of a positive correlation. Oftentimes, negative correlations are desired, such as, perhaps, time spent exercising and money spent on snack cakes. As positive and negative correlations suggest some pattern of association between variables, a correlation coefficient close to zero suggests no relationship. Graphically, such a relationship would look like a horizontal line, suggesting no relationship between the IV and DV. Nonetheless, regardless of correlation value found, one must be thorough in considering whether the correlation value makes theoretical sense—two variables are related that should be related, such as time studying and academic achievement.

Furthermore, although correlations indicate some association between variables, they do not infer causation. When interpreting correlations, it is critical to evaluate the variables being evaluated for association (e.g., how they are measured, reliability) and whether the reported correlation makes theoretical sense. Addressing factors that may challenge the correlation between variables provides a basis to ensure that the association between variables is not spurious or due to some other variable(s).

Chi Square and T-Tests

As discussed above, correlations measure the relationships between variables. Thus, when the variables being compared are nominal or ordinal, the most appropriate test would be a chi square. In essence, a chi square measures the percentages where the variables are correlated. For example, if you are looking at gender (male and female) in relationship to academic level (freshman, sophomore, junior, senior), one would create a 2 × 4 table and look at the percentages of males versus females within the cell at each academic level, thus showing the relationship between the two variables.

However, if you are interested in gender and grade point average (a continuous variable), then you would use a T-Test since you would be interested in which gender has the higher grade point.

Chi square and T-Test are good statistical tests when comparing two variables; however, in most instances a study will be comparing multiple variables. Simply stated, when needing to perform multiple chi squares, it might be best to use a multiple regression, and when having to conduct multiple T-Tests, then an Analysis of Variance (ANOVA) might be the statistical test preferred.

This volume does not permit expansion into the massive variety of statistical tests available to use, but only simply introduces what they are and how they might be used.

Test	Dependent Variable	Independent Variable
frequency	all variable types	all variable types
mean	interval/ratio	interval/ratio
median	all variable types	all variable types
mode	all variable types	all variable types
------------------	------------------	------------------
T-Test*	interval/ratio	nominal (2 categories)
Chi square test	nominal or ordinal (2 or more categories)	nominal or ordinal (2 or more categories)
ANOVA*	interval/ratio	nominal or ordinal (3 or more categories)
Regression	nominal or ordinal (3 or more categories)	nominal or ordinal (3 or more categories)

Adapted from Weinbach and Grinnel (1995), *Statistics for Social Workers*, 3rd ed. White Plains, NY: Longman Publishers.

*ANOVA (Analysis of Variance) produces the same type of results as performing multiple T-Tests. However, one cannot perform multiple T-Tests. ANOVA looks at both the between-group differences as well as the within-group differences, meaning it is a useful statistical test for small sample sizes.

Instruments and Data Collection worksheet

The next two pages provide you with a format to list your variables, data source, and their attributes. There may be times when the instruments may be a pre-existing test or intake form, or you may choose to design your own source, as in a semi-structured interview schedule. Whatever you choose, it is important to identify the attributes of the variable and your data source. There may be times when you identify the same variable but will be gathering data from different sources, as identified above with the variable, "reasons for being homeless."

INSTRUMENTS AND DATA SOURCES

State your hypothesis or question_____

_____

Identify your variable, how you plan to gather the information about the variable (data source), and the attributes of the variable within that data source.

Variable	Data Source	Attributes
_____	_____	_____
		_____
		_____
		_____
		_____
_____	_____	_____
		_____
		_____
_____	_____	_____
		_____
		_____

_____   _____   _____

                                                  _____

                                                  _____

                                                  _____

For items above that do not have readily available instruments, identify the characteristics of the instrument you plan to use. For example, if you plan to use a semi-structured interview, list the questions you want covered.

Proposed Instrument(s)   Critical Characteristics (for ex: type of instrument
                                          and how it will be administered, etc.)

                                          _____

_____   _____

                                          _____

                                          _____

                                          _____

_____   _____

                                          _____

_____   _____

                                          _____

Instrument reliability and validity

For each instrument selected or proposed in the above two sections, how reliable and valid are these instruments?

Reliability: How closely do repeated observations (by different people, at different times, etc.) of the same thing agree with each other?

Validity: With what assurance do we know that the instrument is measuring what we believe it is measuring?

	Instrument	Reliability	Validity
1.	_____	_____	_____
		_____	_____
2.	_____	_____	_____
		_____	_____
3.	_____	_____	_____

Code Books

Data Collection Forms—Code Book

It is one thing to have instruments for data, but it is another to understand how you are going to organize your data once you have collected it. The organization of data is crucial if you are going to be able to make some sense out of the information you have collected. Some data is easy to organize; for example, surveys are designed to answer particular questions. The values used for each variable creates what is called a **code book.** Therefore, the data on closed-ended questions can be quantified and entered into a statistical computer program. Programs like SPSS (Statistical Package for the Social Sciences) have built-in code books when you enter in each variable name and the specific values. However, there are a number of programs that will provide some statistical information, such as a basic spreadsheet program like Excel, that does not have a built-in code book function. Therefore, it is important to build a code book to make sense of the meaning of each of the values of each of the variables. For example, the homeless shelter intake form provided the staff with a menu of reasons why people may be homeless. Each item on the menu would be assigned a numerical value to be entered into the computer. The computer reads the numbers, but it is important to have a code book that will assist you in translating the meaning of those numbers.

Other data, such as qualitative data, is harder to organize. This will be discussed in the next chapter, but in essence, interviews will need to be read and reread to determine if there are specific themes that emerge. Then a decision is made to see if that theme relates to a variable in your study. Once generalized themes are identified, then values can be assigned to differentiate variances within the themes.

For example, a code book from the homeless shelter intake form might look like this:

Reason left last address:
    1 = evicted
    2 = family problems
    3 = jail release
    4 = no money
    5 = substance abuse
    6 = move/in transit
    9 = missing

Reason for needing shelter
    1 = nowhere else to go
    2 = evicted from residence
    3 = no money/income
    4 = referred by individual or social services
    9 = missing

The data would be entered into a spreadsheet or organized in a chart that might look like:

category	Total pop	shelter 1	shelter 2
reason left last address			
Eviction	n (%)	n (%)	n (%)
Family problem	n (%)	n (%)	n (%)
Jail release	n (%)	n (%)	n (%)
No money	n (%)	n (%)	n (%)
Substance abuse	n (%)	n (%)	n (%)
Move/in transit	n (%)	n (%)	n (%)

(n is the number of cases for each category followed by the percent of the total.)

DATA COLLECTION FORMS

State your hypothesis_____

_____

Use the space below to sketch forms you will use to record the data from your study. Alternatively, you may list and describe the forms below and then attach specimens. For example, if you are using a survey, attach a copy of the survey. If you plan to use an interview, attach a copy of the interview schedule you plan to use. In doing a survey or even using an intake form that is measurable, it is helpful to create a code book and a partially completed coded data sheet. For example, a codebook would identify:

        var1   values 1 =
                            2 =
                            3 =

        var2   values 1 =
                            2 =
                            3 =

This would be organized in a chart that would look like:

            1   2   3

        var1   _____
        var2   _____

CH. 12

Qualitative Data

The last chapter provided data analysis techniques used in quantitative research that looks at causal inferences between independent and dependent variables—in other words, how the independent variable affects the dependent variable. In some cases, it is possible to manipulate the independent variable to obtain a different outcome with the dependent variable. In other instances, it is the comparison of multiple independent variables to see the differing effects that they have on the dependent variable. In all of these cases, it is a matter of understanding a causal relationship between variables with the independent variable having some type of cause on the dependent variable.

Quantitative research explains an observation and uses various statistical methods in order to explain what is being observed. As such, it is important to have the data coded as nominal, ordinal, or continuous data. Once the type of data being used is identified, it is possible to determine the type of measurement that will be used to explain the relationship. If the data is continuous, then it is possible to use a measure of central tendency to explain the observation. If the data is not continuous, then correlational measures will be used to see how one variable relates to the other. Regardless, the analyses of these statistical tests produce an "r" score. When the "r" score is multiplied by itself, it produces what is classified as an "r^2," meaning how much of the interaction between the two variables can be explained by the interaction itself and not by chance. Statistically then, the "r^2" value is located on a probability table to determine, based on the degrees of freedom (the number of cases studies less one), whether the value has a level of significance at the 95 percent (depicted as < .05) or better or the 99 percent (depicted as < .01) or better. In much of social science research, an r^2 value of .20 or greater will show a level of significance at the 95 percent level or better.

This raises some questions about what is happening the other 80 percent of the time. However, quantitative research is solely looking at the relationship between the two variables to see if there is some significance. If there is the burning question to understand the dynamic of the other 80 percent of the time, then one will have to turn to **qualitative research** methods to gain a deeper understanding.

To gain the r^2 results, quantitative research relies primarily on some type of experimental or quasi-experimental design. In addition, it is looking at large numbers or samples that are potentially generalizable to the larger population to explain the relationship. Since it is impossible to sample the entire population, a portion of the population is tested, and it is hypothesized that the

139

results relate to the larger population since it was very purposeful to select a sample that could be generalized to the larger population.

Thus, quantitative research is a very specific way to measure the relationship between independent and dependent variables. It is solely interested in that particular relationship and not the intervening factors. Therefore, quantitative research may demonstrate that a relationship that is effective only 20 percent of the time may be significant, but it does not explain the other 80 percent. If you are interested in understanding the other factors, then it is important to look at some qualitative research. There are times when researchers will conduct both qualitative and quantitative research methods in the same study; this is called **mixed methods research** and was discussed in chapter 8.

In essence, qualitative research is exploring or seeking to understand relationships between variables. In most instances, it is the social condition or the dependent variable that is evident and one wants to understand what factors are contributing to the observed outcome. Thus, where quantitative research may be looking at cause and effect between independent and dependent variables, qualitative research works backward in that you see the effect but are searching for the cause.

To understand cause, it is important to understand sources of data where one can determine whether it is a source or not. Therefore, qualitative research relies heavily on non-numerical sources of information and the analysis of meaning of those sources. The nature of these sources and how they are analyzed will be discussed below.

Patterns of Discovery

Qualitative research as a mechanism for discovery has been used by various disciplines and has existed as a primary source of inquiry by those disciplines. Social anthropologists have used the idea of ethnography as a method of learning about different cultures. Many of the techniques used by anthropologists have been adapted into what we currently classify as qualitative research.

Based on an ethnographic concept, Hammersley and Atkinson (1984) looked at ethnographic methods as a way of collecting data. They raised a question as to whether the researcher can be purely objective in the observation and not be influenced by the researcher's values. These types of questions have been raised questions about the validity of qualitative research. Thus, there are many quantitative researchers who for years discounted qualitative research as a sound, viable method of discovery. However, more recently, it is gaining greater acceptance as a source of inquiry. For example, there was a time when there was minimal federal funding for qualitative research methods, unless the researcher's name was Erwin Goffman. However, now people recognize the value of qualitative research in building theory to help explain social conditions in society.

Part of that theory development process in qualitative research emerged from the work of Glaser and Strauss, who coined the term "grounded theory" in 1967. The term was based on the fact that there were few to no social theories that could be classified as grand theories. A grand theory is one that can explain an observation most of the time (like gravity). Thus, within the social sciences, there are a number of mid-range theories that can predict outcomes only a mid-range of the time, hence the reason for seeing an r^2 at 20 percent as being significant. Thus, Glaser and Strauss created the technique called grounded theory where an individual will continue to collect data about a particular social condition until data saturation has occurred. Data saturation is defined as a period when the data that has been collected begins to be repetitive. In reality, most qualitative researchers do not have the time or resources to collect data until data saturation is reached; therefore, the researcher(s) may arbitrarily identify a sample size that can be investigated in a timely manner within the available resources.

This raises the question of where is this sample drawn? This is where the importance of research question comes into focus. Since the research question should drive the situation to be investigated. Then it is important to identify who are the best subjects to understand that social condition to answer the question. Flanagan (1954), through his Critical Incident Technique, identified that each person is an expert of his/her experience. Thus, once the population best suited to answer your question is identified, Flanagan (1954) would treat each individual within that population as an expert of his or her own experience. Thus, each researcher should treat each subject as an expert and then analyze that data by looking at the information shared from an expert in that social condition. The researcher would then look at a variety of similar experts in that social condition and identify the similarities and commonalities between these different experts. These common themes or threads are the beginning of the process of identifying patterns that may help explain the social condition.

Looking for Patterns

The goal of qualitative research is to identify factors that contribute to a social condition that can be called patterns. Lofland and Lofland (1995) struggled with how to determine a pattern or not. They identified six categories that a researcher can use in order to categorize a pattern. These categories are: the frequency that the factor was identified as a contributing condition to the social condition; the magnitude that the factor relates to contributing to the social condition; how the factor is structured in its relationship to the social condition; the process that the factor used in addressing the social condition; the causal relationship between the factor and the social condition; and the outcome or consequence of that particular factor.

Now that there are categories for understanding the observations, there is still the question of the analysis. Miles and Huberman (1994) said that there are two ways of analyzing the observation. One method would be to look at the variables generated by the various sources within the sample and to link them as common themes. A second way is to look at each case or subject and identify all the various themes that relate to a particular social condition. In essence, a combination of the two is used. Each case identifies all the factors that relate to a particular condition from his/her framework. Then these are coded into variable themes and are compared. Hence, this is a way of triangulating the data between various sources in order to achieve higher levels of validity of the themes that emerge.

Sources of data

Since qualitative research relies on non-numeric data, there are various sources that can be used to gain understanding of meaning about a social condition. Probably the most widely identified are interviews and/or focus groups. This is when the researcher goes directly to the subject and asks some directed questions to gain a deeper understanding from the subject's perspective about the social condition.

Observation is another tool that is used to gather data. There are a variety of observation techniques that are being used. Some include videotaping, while others involve use of a one-way mirror. In any instance, observation is purely observing with no interaction. Hence, this differs from participant observation, where the researcher is actively engaged in the research observation process. Some raise questions about this process, as the researcher can actually be influencing the results just because of the presence and/or interaction of the researcher with the subjects.

Much of historical research is also qualitative. In these instances, the researcher is identifying original records or transcripts and analyzing them to gain a new understanding about the social condition at the time. For example, by understanding the creation of the Weedpatch School during the 1930s "Dust Bowl" era, it was important to look at the historical records of the transcripts of the school board to understand the reluctance of the Kern School District to permit the "Oakies" into the existing schools. Since none of the existing schools wanted to accept those individuals who had migrated from Oklahoma and Texas because it was felt that they were backward, a new school, the Weedpatch School, was created to address the educational needs of the migrant children living in the Weedpatch area of Kern County, California. Subsequently, the Weedpatch School became one of the model schools in the area, providing vocational education services and also providing the first public swimming pool in Kern County. It was a little ironic that the discrimination faced by those migrating to Weedpatch contributed to a rallying point for those residents to surpass the expectations of the residential population at that time.

Collecting Interview/Focus Group Data

As mentioned above, interview and focus groups are the most commonly used sources of qualitative data. However, there is a process or a system that should be followed in order to guide the interview. This is called an **interview schedule**. The interview schedule is based upon the gaps in the current level of information that is available to explain the particular social condition that is being explored. As such, the cases or sample selection is chosen since it represents experts or persons from whom it is important to gain a perspective about their understanding of the social condition. Since the goal is to identify information about the gaps within existing information, it is important to develop an interview schedule that consists of open-ended questions that will allow the subjects to share their experiences. Hence the questions in the interview schedule can guide the interview but need to be open enough where the subject can express him/herself openly and freely to be able to use his/her experience to explain the social condition. It is from hearing about the subject's experiences that themes emerge. These themes are compared with other subjects in order to triangulate the data and achieve a level of validity of the information that can later be tested through quantitative means.

Since it is important to be cognizant of the time of the interview, it is suggested to keep the interview schedule short, between five and seven questions. As just mentioned, time is very important, and an interview with a single subject should be planned for about an hour. A focus group where there may be eight to twelve people should be planned for about an hour and a half.

Analysis

Analysis of qualitative data is the hard part since it is looking at responses from different subjects or cases and identifying any common themes that may emerge. Thus, interviews and focus groups are audio taped (after obtaining human subject consent) and then each of the audio tapes is reviewed to ascertain if themes emerge. To check on the coding validation, if there is more than one researcher, then there is the need to check the themes using some inter-rater reliability factors to ascertain whether each researcher identified the theme the same way the other researchers did. If not, then there is a need for researchers to arrive at a consensus about the meaning of the experience and how it should be rated in relationship to the theme.

As the themes emerge, they are compared by the experiences and themes that other subjects shared. The commonality between the various subjects provides validity to the theme and is called a constant comparative process, since there is a constant comparison between the various subjects.

Another way of analyzing qualitative data is by creating a concept map. Concept mapping is a dynamic tool that is used by looking at how subjects describe the cause-and-effect relationship when explaining the particular social condition from his/her perspective.

Thus, in explaining the qualitative research process, one says that it is easier on the front part of the research process since the researcher is exploring for causal relationships, but it is a lot more time-consuming on the analysis end of the research process since it is identifying themes from various sources of subjects. As such, the sample size within qualitative research studies is smaller to be able to analyze the data more closely. Even with the advent of qualitative data computer-assisted tools, the process of analyzing the data can be tedious.

Qualitative data analysis is very different from quantitative data analysis and relies on a combination of art and science in the analysis process. Unlike quantitative data that comes from using statistics and the numbers generated by the statistics to measure confidence levels of the interactions based on those numbers, qualitative data is a **non-numeric approach** to data analysis. As such, qualitative data comes from various sources, including, but not exclusive to: interviews, focus groups, historical records, meeting minutes, ethnographies, observations, or speech content. As you can see from this list, almost anything can be used as a source of qualitative data to be analyzed.

The analysis of qualitative data is where the blending of art and science comes into play. It is important to have a clear understanding of the theoretical concepts that are being tested or explored. This should then lead to some generalizable observations that you are hoping to identify in your data sources. Examples of these generalizable observations would be identified within the data source and would be called implicit assumptions that would lead to themes that can then be used as tools to code other examples from the data. Here is the tricky part, because some of the examples in the data may support the assumption, whereas others may be contradictory to it. Both are important and become a point where the data needs to be highlighted to assist in understanding the meaning. It also lends itself to the creation of subthemes within the large theme or even possibly a separate theme to be explored. Before the advent of computers, this was called a cutting-and-pasting process, and many times, qualitative researchers would have shoe boxes filled with various notes representing the themes that have been identified by the data. With the advent of computer-generated software, the process of cutting and pasting continues to exist; however, now it is done electronically rather than by hand. In addition, there are times when a piece of data could be classified as addressing two different themes, which would necessitate placing it in both places. The coding of the data is where the art and science take place, as it is dependent upon the researcher's application of the theory while interpreting the data and the coding of it accordingly. Some of this can be exemplified by concept mapping or mapping.

Mapping

Mapping or knowledge mapping is a process used in medical education for metacognition, a useful tool in trying to understand complex issues. On the one hand, it is similar to the analogy that a picture is worth a thousand words, where one would pictorially look at the interrelationship between various concepts, finding it easier to present the content in this fashion rather than through massive text. The reality is that using figures and diagrams to represent the meaning of things is something that we already do.

The language used in concept mapping is similar to the language used in some of the current qualitative software programs. These include terms such as: nodes or characteristics and parts and links for arrows and directions.

As stated, there have been various types of software packages that have been developed for use in qualitative data analysis. Since qualitative data is coded based on a cut-and-paste method, the software replicates that process electronically. The process can be somewhat tedious and dependent upon interpretation. What is important to know is that the packages are developed on a database software format. That means that once you enter the data into a category, it is organized and stored based on that category. It is like having multiple folders in your word processing software that stores the various pieces of data. The advantage to database software over folders in word processing software is that the data is interactive within the database software, whereas folders in word processing are not. As a tangent, some of my students have stated that they have used the qualitative software package as a way of keeping track of their literature when doing their research projects. They have found that entering the article or book and organizing it around themes makes it easier when having to write the paper because they can pull the theme and have a quick list of all the references that relate to that particular theme.

Just to mention some of the different qualitative software packages from a historical perspective will provide some context as to how the software has developed. The very first one was Ethnograph.

It was not written in a Windows format and did basic cutting and pasting of a transcribed interview. Then came HyperQual and Hyper Research, which took the stored coded data and counted each entry so it could be converted into a statistical analysis software program. NUD*IST, or **N**on-numerical **U**nstructured **D**ata **I**ndexing **S**earching and **T**heorizing, was developed in the 1990s to automate some of the work associated with qualitative data analysis by auto-coding signified text data, importing table data, and using command files to regulate analysis processes. The developer of NUD*IST is QSR, and they eventually transformed it to NVIVO and its closest competitor, ATLAS.ti. These packages are both Windows and Mac compatible and have expanded the scientific aspects of qualitative data analysis. Using the software does not eliminate the need for coding the data, though. The software packages are good tools for organizing the data once you have coded it.

Qualitative data analysis is not the same as quantitative data analysis. The nature of the data is different, and it is important to recognize that how the data is analyzed is very different. Most importantly, it is imperative to realize that you are dealing with non-numeric data. As such, there is the need to understand the art and science relationship that takes place in qualitative data analysis.

Reporting Results

Whether you are a burgeoning researcher or a student needing to write a research paper, it is important to understand how to report your findings. Reporting your results is important because it is one thing to personally gain knowledge from the study, but it is important to share it. As a student, it is important to share the information for a grade, and as a researcher, it is important to share the findings as a way to further the knowledge about the question you asked. If nothing is done with the information, then there is no benefit to others. This addresses the proverbial question, "If a tree falls in the forest and no one heard it, did the tree actually fall?" That is the same thing with research. If you do a study and then do not report the results, then has anyone gained from the information acquired? Therefore, it is important to plan to report the results of your study, regardless of whether you have found new information or not.

There is a systematic process used by all researchers in reporting results. This is important because as you are also a consumer of research, you will notice the format that is being used to report the results. By understanding the format, it will help you also become a better consumer of the written research. The logical process used to present one's findings is very systematic.

Journal Article Outline

The basic format used to report findings is also the form that is used when the research is presented in a journal article. The format is as follows:

1. Abstract
2. Introduction
   a. Statement of the problem
   b. Review of the literature
   c. Specific statement of the research questions
3. Method
   a. Participants
   b. Materials
   c. Dependent variables
   d. Procedure

4. Results
5. Discussion
6. References

---

adapted from Huck (2008) *Reading Statistics and Research,* 5th ed. Boston, MA: Allyn & Bacon.

The abstract is a short synopsis of the study. It includes the research question, the sample and the methodology used to obtain the data, a summary of the data, and then a brief introduction of the discussion with next steps. The abstract is usually about 250 words long and should be written after the entire study has been written, as the abstract is a summary of the study. A more detailed description of the abstract and how to read it in relationship to its relevance appeared in Chapter 3 when describing how to develop the literature review.

The introduction is either written as one section or sometimes split between the problem and the literature review. Regardless, the beginning of the introduction is a bold statement of the problem; it addresses your interest in conducting the study. Then the literature review provides the supporting evidence, as found by other authors/researchers, to help build your argument. It is also important to identify the theoretical context that is being used to help understand the rationale for how you are looking at the problem and begins to provide a road map for the methodology that will be used to collect data. This section ends with a list of the specific questions or hypotheses that you hope to answer in the study. If this section is split between problem statement and literature review, the literature review section will be longer since it includes the theoretical context for how you are looking at the problem and the supporting evidence from other researchers, ending with your research questions.

The methodology section is next. This usually begins with a statement about answering the questions that you mentioned above, followed by the plan of your data collection, including your sample and whatever psychometric measurement tools you would be using. If you are conducting a qualitative study, you might even provide your interview schedule and how the questions will help to answer your research questions. The same for mixed methods research in that you would explain both the quantitative and qualitative aspects of the study with the rationale on how the findings will be used to answer the research questions.

The results section is the reporting of the data. If quantitative data, it would most likely include copies of the statistical tables of the tests that you used with a description of the findings, i.e., the statistic showed significance at either the .05 or .01 levels or not. If you are presenting qualitative data, it is helpful to identify the themes that emerged and then include supporting statements to show how those statements relate to the themes.

To this point, the research report is very much factual with very little opinion as to what it means. Your opinion is relegated to the discussion section. It is this section where you build on the questions using the data that you provided and answer the "So what?" question. This is where you provide a discussion of the data and how the data can be used to answer the research questions. Once you have provided that part of the discussion, then you need to provide a section on the limitations to the study, i.e., it is only a sample of the population and may not be generalizable to the entire population, or something to that effect. The last part of the study addresses two areas: first, next steps in continuing to answer the questions, and second, implications for practice.

When thinking about next steps, it is important to think about what action should be taken. This is an important component of all the types of action research such as participatory action research (PAR) or community-based participatory research (CBPR). If working with community groups, there are a number of tools that can be used to assist in the planning of the action steps. This might involve a Force Field Analysis or a logic model.

Force Field Analysis

Simply stated, a Force Field Analysis is a visual diagram that identifies the problem in the middle, the stakeholders at the top, the driving forces for a change, and the restraining forces preventing the change on either side, culminating with the action steps to be taken at the bottom. Here is a diagram of a Force Field Analysis.

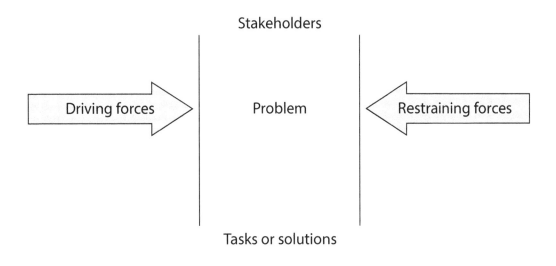

FIGURE 13.1 FORCE FIELD ANALYSIS

Logic Model

A logic model is a tool that identifies the resources that are needed to take action (inputs); what steps will be taken to achieve the action (activities); the quantifiable changes that will occur such as providing services to x number of people (outputs); and then the goals that will be addressed (outcomes). Some logic models are broken into beginning, middle, and end outcomes to demonstrate the ongoing nature of the project. However, represented below is the simplest form of a logic model.

Inputs	Activities	Outputs	Outcomes

FIGURE 13.2 LOGIC MODEL

There are a variety of other tools that could be used to assist in developing action steps for the next steps of the research project. Many times, these are important when writing grant proposals.

The final section of the report is a listing of all the references used. Most social science research uses the APA (Publication Manual of the American Psychological Association) formatting. Thus, your references have been identified in text with author and date with the full reference appearing in the reference section.

A quick word about writing the results of your study. As discussed above, the social sciences consist of a number of mid-range theories that may only explain 20 percent of the relationships. Therefore, there is probably some value in submitting your work for publication as it could possibly expand the knowledge in the field.

REPORTING OF RESULTS

State your hypothesis_____

_____.

In the space below, provide a comprehensive outline of how you will present your results. Make sure to include all the components of a research study that were identified above.

Conclusion

You have now completed the steps in conducting a research project. Regardless of whether your study is qualitative, quantitative, or mixed-methods, the steps are similar. One type may emphasize certain areas over others; for example, quantitative research is more applicable to statistical analysis than qualitative, while qualitative research relies on you to develop different mechanisms for organizing and analyzing data, and mixed-methods will use both. However, the essence of the steps is the same. This book was designed to take the mystery out of the research process by breaking research into manageable parts. Once you have completed the steps outlined above, it is important to share the knowledge you have gained with your colleagues. Refer back to the section on reporting results for an outline of how research articles appear in the journals.

The important thing to remember is that research is part of everything that you do as a worker. Even when working with client systems of any size, whenever you begin an assessment, you are inputting the data into your data banks to see whether that information is generalizable to other situations that you have been exposed to. Research is only a concept used to define how we organize and analyze information. So have a good time and enjoy your research.

References

Agresti, A. & Finlay, B. (1986). *Statistical methods for the social sciences.* San Francisco, CA: Dellen.

Allen-Meares, P. & Lane, B.A. (1990). Social work practice: Integrating qualitative and quantitative data collection techniques. *Social work, 35*(5), p. 452–458.

Anastas, J.W. & MacDonald, M.L. (1994). *Research design for social work and human services.* New York: Lexington Books.

Arkava, M.I. & Lane, T.A. (1983). *Beginning social work research.* Boston: Allyn & Bacon.

Ary, D., Jacobs, L. C., & & Sorensen, C. (2002). *Introduction to research in education (6th ed.).* Belmont, CA: Wadsworth.

Barlow, D.H. & Hersen, M. (2009). *Single case experimental design strategies for studying behavior change* (3rd ed.) Boston: Pearson/Allyn & Bacon.

Berg, B.L. (2004) *Qualitative research methods for the social sciences (5th ed.)* Boston: Pearson/Allyn & Bacon.

Bernstein, I. H., & Nunnally, J. C. (1994). *Psychometric theory.* New York: McGraw-Hill.

Berger, P.L. & Luckman, T. (1966). *The social construction of reality.* New York: Anchor Books.

Bickman, L & Rog, DJ (2009) *The Sage Handbook of Applied Research Methods* (2nd ed.). Los Angeles: Sage.

Bisman, C. D., & Hardcastle, D. A. (1999). *Integrating research into practice: A model for effective social work.* Belmont, CA: Brooks/Cole.

Bisman, C. D., & Hardcastle, D. A. (1999). A model for using research methodologies in practice. *Journal of Teaching in Social Work, 19*(1/2), 47–63.

Bloom, M., & Britner, P. A. (2012). *Client-centered evaluation: New models for helping professionals.* Boston: Allyn & Bacon.

Bloom, M., Fischer, J., & Orme, J. G. (1999). *Evaluating practice: Guidelines for the accountable professional.* Boston: Allyn & Bacon.

Bloom, M., & Orme, J. (1993). Ethics and single-system design. *Journal of Social Service Research, 18*(1/2), 161–180.

Bogo, M., Regehr, C., Hughes, J., Power, R., & Globerman, J. (2002). Evaluating a measure of student field performance in direct service: Testing reliability and validity of explicit criteria. *Journal of Social Work Education, 38*(3), 385–401.

Bride, B. E. (2001). Single-gender treatment of substance abuse: Effect on treatment retention and completion. *Social Work Research, 24*(4), 222–231.

Bronson, D.E. & Blythe, B.J. (1987). Computer support for single case evaluation of practice. *Social Work Research and Abstracts, 24*(2), p. 21–22.

Campbell, D.T. & Stanley, J.C. (2015). *Experimental and Quasi-Experimental Designs for Research.* Ravenio Books.

Cheek, J. (2011). The Politics and Practices of Funding Qualitative Inquiry: messages about messages about messages. ... In N. K. Denzin & Y. S. Lincoln (eds.) *The Sage Handbook of Qualitative Research.* (pp. 251–268). Los Angeles, CA: Sage.

Cohen, D. (2002). Research on the drug treatment of schizophrenia: A critical appraisal and implications for social work education. *Journal of Social Work Education, 38*(2), 217–239.

Conboy, A., Auerbach, C., Schnall, D., & LaPorte, H. H. (2000). MSW student satisfaction with using single-system-design computer software to evaluate social work practice. *Research on Social Work Practice, 10*(1), 127–138.

Comer, E. W., & Fraser, M. W. (1998). Evaluation of six family-support programs: Are they effective? Families in Society: *The Journal of Contemporary Human Services, 79*(2), 134–148.

Corcoran, K. & Fischer, J. (2013) *Measures for Clinical Practice and Research* (Vols. 1& 2). New York: Oxford University Press.

Creswell, J. W. (1994). Qualitative and quantitative approaches. *Qualitative and quantitative approaches.* New York: Sage Publications, Inc.

Creswell, J.W. (2015) *A Concise introduction to mixed methods research.* Los Angeles, CA: Sage Publications, Inc.

Davis, E. D. (1992). Reconsidering the use of race as an explanatory variable in program evaluation. *New Directions in Program Evaluation, 53,* 55–67.

De Anda, D. (2001). A qualitative evaluation of a mentor program for at-risk youth: The participants' perspective. *Child and Adolescent Social Work Journal, 18*(2), 97–117.

De Poy, E. & Gilson, S.F. (2003). *Evaluation practice: Thinking and action principles for social work practice.* Pacific Grove, CA: Brooks/Cole-Thomson Learning.

Derezotes, D. (2000). Evaluation of yoga & meditation trainings with adolescent sex offenders. *Child and Adolescent Social Work Journal, 17,* 97–111.

Dillman, D. A. (1972) Increasing mail questionnaire response in large samples of the general public. *The Public Opinion Quarterly, 36*(2), p. 254–257.

Ducharme, F., LeVasque, L., Gendron, M., & Legault, A. (2001). Development process and qualitative evaluation of a program to promote the mental health of family caregivers. *Clinical Nursing Research, 10,* 182–202.

Fanshel, D., Marsters, P. A., Finch, S. J., & Grundy, J. F. (1992). Strategies for the analysis of databases in social service systems. In A. J. Grasso, & I. Epstein (Eds.), *Research utilization in the social services* (pp. 301–323). New York, NY: Haworth Press.

Faulkner, SS & Faulkner CA (2014) *Research Methods for Social Workers: A Practice-Based Approach.* Chicago: Lyceum Books, Inc.

Field, A. (2009) *Discovering Statistics Using SPSS* (3rd ed.). Los Angeles: Sage.

Flanagan, J.C. (1954). The Critical Incident Technique. *Psychological Bulletin, 54*(4), 1–33.

Fortune, A. E., Briar-Lawson, K., & McCallion, P. (2010). *Social work practice for the 21st century.* New York: Columbia University Press. (eBook, CSUB library)

Friedman, B.D. (1994). No place like home: A study of two homeless shelters. *Journal of Social Distress and the Homeless, 3*(4) , 321–340.

Friedman, B.D. & Levine-Holdowsky, M. (1997). Overcoming barriers to homeless delivery services: A community response. *Journal of Social Distress and the Homeless, 6*(1), 13–28.

Glaser, B.G. & Strauss, A.L. (1967). *The discovery of grounded theory: Strategies for qualitative research.* New York: Aldine.

Hacker, K. (2013) *Community-Based Participatory Research.* Los Angeles: Sage.

Hammersley, M. & Atkinson, P. (1983) *Ethnography: Principles in Practice.* London: Tavistock.

Hart, P. & Nolan, K. (1999). A Critical Analysis of Research in Environmental Education. *Studies in Science Education, 34*(1), 1–69.

Hasenfeld, Y., & Patti, R. (1992) The utilization of research in administrative practice. In J. Grasso, & I. Epstein (Eds.), *Research utilization in the social services* (pp. 221–234). New York: Haworth Press.

Holden, G., Meenaghan, T., Anastas, J., & Metrey, G. (2002). Outcomes of social work education: The case for social work self-efficacy. *Journal of Social Work Education, 38*(1), 115–133.

Huck, Schuyler W. (2008). *Reading Statistics and Research* (5th ed.). Boston, MA: Allyn & Bacon.

Hudgins, C. A., & Allen-Meares, P. (2000). Translational research: A new solution to an old problem? *Journal of Social Work Education, 36*(1), 2–4.

Kane, R.A. & Kane, R.L. (1981). *Assessing the elderly: A practical guide to measurement.* Lexington, MA: Lexington Books.

Kazi, M. A. F. (1998). *Single case evaluation by social workers.* Aldershot, England: Ashgate.

Kreuger, R. A., & Casey, M. A. (2009). *Focus groups: A practical guide for applied research.* Thousand Oaks, CA: Sage Publications, Inc.

Krueger, R. A., & King, J. A. (1998). *Involving community members in focus groups. Focus Group Kit 5.* Thousand Oaks, CA: Sage Publications, Inc.

Lawson, H.A.; Caringi, J.C.; Pyles, L.; Jurkowski, J.M.; & Bozlak, C.T. (2015). *Participatory Action Research.* New York: Oxford University Press.

Leech, N.L.; Barrett, K.C.; & Morgan, G.A. (2011). *IBM SPSS for Intermediate Statistics: Use and Interpretation* (4th ed.). New York, Routledge.

Lofland, J.L. & Lofland L.H. (1995). *Analyzing social settings: A guide to qualitative observation and analysis.* Belmont, CA: Wadsworth.

Lord, F. M., Novick, M. R., & Birnbaum, A. (1968). *Statistical theories of mental test scores.* Oxford, England: Addison-Wesley.

Maluccio, T. J., & Aldgate, A. (2011). *Improving outcomes for children and families: Finding and using international evidence.* London: Jessica Kingsley Publishers. (eBook, CSUB library)

Marlow, C. (2011). *Research methods for generalist social work* (5th ed.). Belmont, CA: Brooks/Cole.

Marshall, C., & Rossman, G. B. (1999). *Designing qualitative research* (3rd ed.). Thousand Oaks, CA: Sage.

Masi, D. A. (1997). Evaluating employee assistance programs. *Research on Social Work Practice, 7*(3), 378–391.

Mertens, D. M., & Wilson, A. T. (2012). *Program evaluation theory and practice: A comprehensive guide.* New York: Guilford Press. (eBook, CSUB library)

McDowell, C. (1992, Spring). Standardized test and program evaluation: Inappropriate measures in critical times. *New Directions in Program Evaluation, 53,* 45–54.

Miles, M. B., & Huberman, A. M. (1994). *Qualitative data analysis: An expanded sourcebook.* Sage.

Monette, D. R., Sullivan, T. J., DeJong, C. R. (2011). *Applied social research: A Tool for the Human Services* (5th ed.). Belmont, CA: Brooks/Cole.

Montcalm, D., & Royse, D. (2002). *Data analysis for social workers.* Boston: Allyn & Bacon.

Morelli, P. T. T., & Spencer, M. S. (2000). Use and support of multicultural and antiracist education: Research-informed interdisciplinary social work practice. *Social Work, 45*(2), 166–175.

Morgan, G.A., Leech, N.L, Gloeckner, G.W. & Barrett, K.C. (2011). *IBM SPSS for Introductory Statistics Use and Interpretation* (4th ed.). New York: Routledge, Taylor & Francis.

Netting, F. E., & Williams, F. G. (2000). Expanding the boundaries of primary care for elderly people. *Health & Social Work, 25*(4), 233–243.

Nicholson, B. C., Brenner, V., & Fox, R. A. (1999). A community-based parenting program with low-income mothers of young children. *Families in Society: The Journal of Contemporary Human Services, 5–6,* 247–253.

O'Brien, N., McClellan, T., & Alfs, D. (1992). Data collection: Are social workers reliable? *Administration in Social Work, 16,* 89–100.

O'Hare, T. (2005) *Evidence-Based Practices for Social Workers: an interdisciplinary Approach.* Chicago, IL: Lyceum Books, Inc.

Patton, M. Q. (1986). *Utilization-focused evaluation* (2nd ed.). Beverly Hills, CA: Sage.

Poole, D. L., & Colby, I. C. (2002). Do public neighborhood centers have the capacity to be instruments of change in human services? *Social Work, 47*(2), 142–152.

Reamer, F.G. (1989) The affordable housing crisis and social work. *Social Work, 34*(1), 5–9.

Rock, B. D., & Cooper, M. (2000). Social work in primary care: A demonstration student unit utilizing practice research. *Social Work in Health Care, 31*(1), 1–17.

Royse, D., Thyer, B.A., Padgett, D.K., and Logan, T.K. (2010). *Program Evaluation; An Introduction* (5th ed.). Belmont, CA: Thomson.

Rubin, A. & Babbie E. (2014). *Research methods for Social Work* (8th ed.). Belmont, CA: Brooks/Cole.

Sagor, R. (1992) *How To Conduct Collaborative Action Research.* Association for Supervision and Curriculum Development, 1250 N. Pitt St., Alexandria, VA 22314.

Salkind, N. J. (2000). *Exploring research.* Upper Saddle River, NJ: Prentice Hall.

Salkind, N. J. (2000). *Statistics for people who (think they) hate statistics.* Thousand Oaks, CA: Sage.

Soleman H. Abu-Bader (2010). *Advanced & Multivariate Statistical Methods for Social Science Research with a complete SPSS Guide.* Chicago, IL: Lyceum Books, Inc.

Soleman H. Abu-Bader (2011). *Using Statistical Methods in Social Science Research* (2nd Ed.). Chicago, IL: Lyceum Books, Inc.

Soliman, H. H., Raymond, A., & Lingle, S. (1996). An evaluation of community mental health services following a massive natural disaster. *Human Services in the Rural Environment, 20,* 8–13.

Strauss, A., & Corbin, J. (1998). *Basics of qualitative research: Techniques and procedures for developing grounded theory.* Thousand Oaks, CA: Sage.

Tortu, S., Goldsamt, L. A., & Hamid, R. (2002). *Research and service with hidden populations.* Boston: Allyn & Bacon.

Tripodi, T. (1994). *A primer on single-subject designs for clinical social workers.* Washington, DC: NASW Press.

Trochim, W. (2002). *Research Methods Knowledge Base.* Cornell University.

Tsang, A. K. T. (2000). Bridging the gap between clinical practice and research: An integrated practice-oriented model. *Journal of Social Service Research, 26*(4), 69–90.

Verdugo, E. D. (1998). *Practical problems in research methods: A casebook with questions for discussion.* Los Angeles: Pyrczak.

Westerfeld, A., & Dietz, T. J. (2001). *Planning and conducting agency-based research: A workbook for social work students in field placements.* Boston: Allyn & Bacon.

Weinbach, R. W. (2005). *Evaluating social work services and programs.* Boston: Allyn & Bacon.

Williams, C., Cantillon, P., & Cochrane, M. (2001). The clinical and educational experiences of pre-registration house officers in general practice. *Medical Education, 35*(8), 345–351.

CPSIA information can be obtained
at www.ICGtesting.com
Printed in the USA
LVHW012230120919
630881LV00007B/67/P

9 781516 508624